Affiliate Marketing the Right Way:

How to Make Money Online

Authentically *and* Successfully

By Jules Tillman-Amador

© **Copyright Jules Tillman-Amador 2020 - All rights reserved.**

The content contained within this book may not be reproduced, duplicated or transmitted without direct written permission from the author or the publisher.

Under no circumstances will any blame or legal responsibility be held against the publisher, or author, for any damages, reparation, or monetary loss due to the information contained within this book. Either directly or indirectly. You are responsible for your own choices, actions, and results. The use of the information in this book and/or products and/or services we recommend should be based on your own due diligence and you agree that the author and/or publishers are not liable for any success or failure of your business.

Legal Notice: This book is copyright protected. This book is only for personal use. You cannot amend, distribute, sell, use, quote or paraphrase any part, or the content within this book, without the consent of the author or publisher.

Disclaimer Notice: Please note the information contained within this document is for educational and entertainment purposes only. All effort has been executed to present accurate, up to date, and reliable, complete information. No warranties of any kind are declared or implied. Readers acknowledge that the author is not engaging in the rendering of legal, financial, medical or professional advice. The content within this book has been derived from various sources. Please consult a licensed professional before attempting any techniques outlined in this book.

By reading this document, the reader agrees that under no circumstances is the author responsible for any losses, direct or indirect, which are incurred as a result of the use of the information contained within this document, including, but not limited to, — errors, omissions, or inaccuracies.

Earnings Disclaimer: Any presentation of testimonials and case studies about other's experiences are from actual entrepreneurs and are shown as examples of what is possible for informational purposes only. There are several factors that determine a person's success such as hard work and time, and as such I can in no way guarantee that anyone will achieve the same or similar results. Again, the examples, case studies, and testimonials, are simply illustrative of what is possible.

This book is lovingly dedicated to the three most brilliant, powerful, creative, and loving women I know: my mom, Anita, and my daughters, Jazmin and Jesse. If it weren't for each of you, I wouldn't be an entrepreneur, much less the person I am today. I love you all so much.

Table of Contents

Introduction..i
1 – What is Affiliate Marketing?...1
2 - How to do Affiliate Marketing Legally AND Ethically.......15
3 – Is Affiliate Marketing Passive Income?.............................23
4 - Choosing a Niche..32
5 - Finding Affiliate Programs to Apply to.............................49
6 - Affiliate Marketing with a Blog...61
7 – Keywords & SEO Tips and Tools......................................86
8 – Affiliate Marketing with a Blog..99
9 - Highly Effective, Yet Underused Affiliate Ideas.............118
10 - Affiliate Marketing in Email..137
11 - Affiliate Marketing on Pinterest...................................156
12 - Evergreen vs Limited Time Affiliate Promotions........164
13 - Pitfalls to Avoid..182
References..194

Free Book Bonuses

Hello there! Before you start reading I thought I'd let you know there are A LOT of websites, tools, etc. mentioned in this book. Rather than you typing in each one (or searching for them), I put everything in a handy, free PDF that you can get at:

www.ThrivingAffiliates.com/book-gift

It not only includes the links included in this book, but some other free resources and gifts, just for you! I'm so grateful you've chosen to read this book. Now I'll let you get to it...

Introduction

Picture this: you wake up in the morning, without an alarm clock, feeling refreshed and excited to start your day. You're living your life exactly where and how you want to. You work on projects that energize you. You are fulfilled and **HAPPY.**

In fact, your work fills you with so much passion and inspiration, you can't wait to start your days! While everyone else hates Mondays, you look forward to what they'll bring. While others wait in bumper to bumper traffic just to get to the office, your commute is a simple walk right down the hall from your bedroom.

But you like to play, too. Now, because of your business you can travel, try new experiences, meet new people from all over the world, take afternoons off, and generally (and thoroughly) enjoy life. As you were meant to!

Well, I'm here to tell you: affiliate marketing can help you do all of the above.

There are good, honest people doing affiliate

marketing online who make five, even six figures per month. I'm not talking about the dudes in their flashy cars and giant McMansions, but humble, ~~hard~~ *smart* working people with spouses and families. Wanderlusters. People who hated their jobs and used affiliate marketing as a way to escape the 9 to 5 grind. People who lost their jobs and had to figure out how to replace their income. Regular, everyday people just like you and I.

There are others who do it as a side hustle to make an extra few hundred dollars a month. Stay at home parents. College students. Empty Nesters. People who love their jobs but want and/or need some extra income.

No matter what your reason *or* financial goals, I believe that affiliate marketing can help you reach them. And I wrote this book to help teach you how.

Who am I? Well, my name is Jules and I run a blog all about affiliate marketing at www.ThrivingAffiliates.com. (I also have three niche sites... more about those later!) I started my first online business shortly after my second daughter was born: coding websites with one hand while cuddling my baby in the other.

Since then my business has evolved (and yours

might, too!) But in early 2019, I realized that I loved everything about affiliate marketing, and decided to go all in.

You see, I'm an introvert. And even if you're not, I think you'll agree that these are some pretty fantastic perks of an affiliate business:

- I set my own hours
- I get to work on things I love
- I work where I want to (as long as I have Wi-Fi and my laptop!)
- I don't have to create, store, or ship any products
- I don't have to deal with customer service issues
- I don't have to worry about exchanges, refunds or returns
- My income potential is limitless
- I can build several of these businesses and sell them at a hefty profit if I want to
- I don't have to be an "expert", I just need to have a passion
- My start-up costs can be less than $100

- Everything I need to know is freely (or affordably) available online... or in this book!

If that sounds like a business you'd like to be in, too, read on, because I'm about to teach you all about affiliate marketing, and how it can help you reach your own goals, and create success on your terms.

There is one common thing I think everyone includes in their definition of success and that's **freedom.**

If you're looking to create a life and business that gives you freedom, I believe that affiliate marketing is one way you can achieve it. I hope to not only convince you of this in the following pages, but to also give you the ideas, tools, resources, information and inspiration to make it all happen.

What I won't do is promise you fancy Italian sportscars, luxury yachts, or millions of dollars -- although there are certainly people doing affiliate marketing who have those things. But for every one of those people, there are probably hundreds more that earn little to nothing.

That's just the plain truth.

What I'd like to do is help you land somewhere in the middle.

Making maybe a few hundred extra dollars a month, or $2000 to $10,000 monthly, or more. (And if you really want to make those millions, well, you have to start by earning $1 first, and this book can certainly help you with that, and beyond!)

You see, I believe in you. I believe you can make this "affiliate marketing thing" a success.

Why? (Especially since we've never met!?)

Because you've shown a true desire to succeed just by purchasing this book. And once you've read its contents, you'll have the information and tools you need to get started on the road to success.

When you put this information into action you can start to create that dream life into a reality.

Are you ready? *I sure am!*

Before we get to it, however, I do have one favor to ask…

If you like this book, would you please go rate it on Amazon, and/or wherever you purchased it? I would be eternally grateful, as this helps me get this message out to even more people.

Okay, let's get to it, shall we?!

Chapter 1 – What is Affiliate Marketing?

Because you're reading this book, I'm guessing you at least have some idea of what affiliate marketing is. But just in case you don't (or some other reader doesn't), I thought I'd give a brief explanation on what it is, how it works, and some important things to know about it.

So let's start out with the (yes, somewhat dry) Oxford definition:

"A marketing arrangement by which an online retailer pays commission to an external website for traffic or sales generated from its referrals."

While that may be explanation enough for some people, let me share how this works in the online business world.

Let's say Suzy has a blog about parenting twins. Suzy uses a certain brand of diapers that are not only better for the environment, they're actually affordable, especially when buying twice as many diapers than most parents.

Suzy decides to write a blog post about the diapers, and why she likes them so much. She might include photos of her twins in the diapers, playing or sleeping, etc.

But Suzy was smart! She knew that her blog readers could buy the diapers for the very best price on Amazon. And if she linked to the product page on Amazon with her affiliate link through the Amazon Associates Program (Amazon's name for their affiliate program) and her readers click though and buy (either the diapers, something else, or the diapers AND something else) Suzy will get a commission on everything they buy within 24 hours.

(By the way, Amazon has one of the shortest referral periods – also known as "cookies" which I will explain in more detail shortly. Most affiliate programs have cookies that last 30, 60, 90 days or more. Some are even infinite. But because so many people shop at Amazon, you can still earn quite a bit by referring people to them.)

The cool thing is, almost every single shopping site online – or sites that sell anything, really -- have some sort of affiliate program. So no matter what your blog is about, you will be likely to find some that will fit your audience.

The great thing is, affiliate marketing is a win-win (and sometimes even a win-win-win!) situation. It's always win-win because you get to earn commissions by recommending great products (WIN) for a company who is making additional sales with your help (WIN). The third win comes because occasionally the merchants will offer a discount specifically for your readers, so they WIN (beyond just buying the awesome product you recommended), too!

How Do Affiliate Links Work?

No one really knows… Haha! Just kidding! Basically they work like this:

You sign up for an affiliate program and they give you a special URL or "link" that tracks when someone clicks on it and then goes on to purchase something.

The tracking is done with something called "cookies". (Why they named them that, I have no idea!?) When it comes to the Internet (and not the sweets your mom used to bake for you) cookies are simply small files sent from a website, stored on a person's computer that hold data about the websites (and other information) that person visited.

Cookies can be blocked or cleared, but most people these days understand they are just part of the Internet experience. And why, after looking up hammers on HomeDepot.com you'll see an ad for hammers in your Facebook feed later that day or week. (That's called "re-targeting" and let me tell you, it works! Which is why you see it happen so often.) Yes, it can feel a little stalker-ish at times, but it can also be helpful for both users and businesses.

In relationship to affiliate marketing, you'll frequently hear about cookie length. Different affiliate programs have different cookie lengths, as I mentioned above.

For example, Target's cookie length is 7 Days. Etsy's cookie length is 30 days. And SiteGround (the website hosting company I use and am an affiliate for) has a 60 day cookie. Some will go even longer, but I'd say the length I see most often is 30 days.

You may be wondering: what if someone clicks my

affiliate link (that has, say, a 30 day cookie) and then they click on someone else's affiliate link 5 days later? Well, that depends!

Some companies lock your cookie for the entire 30 days (or whatever the cookie length is). Others use a "last clicked" policy, which means that if that person clicked your link first and another blogger's link after and then they buy something, the other blogger gets the commission. It can feel like a bummer, for sure. So just be sure you know each program's rules and terms.

What is Deep Linking?

Depending on the business itself, some affiliate programs will simply give you links to their home page, and or a specific sales page (or pages).

But deep linking comes in handy when a site has tens, or even millions of products. Because a "deep link" is an affiliate link to one specific product or page on a website.

Not all affiliate programs offer deep linking. But, in my opinion, the smart ones do!

For instance, I'm an affiliate for a company called

Creative Market. I have a deep link on my site that leads to their freebies page, where they offer 6 new free digital goods every Monday.

Of course, I don't earn commissions when people click through and grab the free stuff. But because of Creative Market's generous one year cookie length and the fact that they offer so many high quality items, I feel confident sending people to the freebies page because once they see everything they can buy there, they usually come back and purchase items, too.

That's just one of many ways you can use deep links. Obviously, in the example above with Suzy and her diaper recommendation, she would use a deep link directly to the brand of diapers she liked best, not to the Amazon.com homepage, hoping the person who clicked through would a). remember the brand name, etc., and b). even bother to type it into the search bar.

As you can see, deep linking is vital to you making more affiliate sales and commissions.

Types of Affiliate Programs

In general, there are two types of affiliate programs:

individual and network. An example of an individual affiliate program is Amazon. (I know I use Amazon as a frequent example, but that is because it's not only one of the most popular out there, but it's also the affiliate program most bloggers start with.)

So to sign up to Amazon's affiliate program you would simply go to their website, scroll to the very bottom and click on "Become an Affiliate" (at the time of the publication of this book. It might say something slightly different, like "Associates Program", etc.)

But say you want to sign up for Etsy's affiliate program. Well, they run theirs through an "affiliate network" called AWIN. So you have to sign up to be in the network (AWIN) first, and then join Etsy's affiliate program.

Networks like AWIN (as well as others like ShareASale, MaxBounty, CJ.com, etc.) handle the affiliate programs for multiple, sometimes hundreds or even thousands of different businesses.

What I like about networks is that you (generally) only have to enter your information once. Most affiliate programs will require your name, address, tax ID (EIN or Social Security number in the US), your blog name, a description of your blog, and sometimes traffic and social media stats and even how you plan on promoting their products.

So if you're signing up for more than one affiliate program, networks make that easy because they store and share that information with the companies you apply with.

How You Get Paid

Of course, I'm sure you want to know how (and how much!) you get paid for referring customers via affiliate programs. Well, not only will the amount vary, but so will the way in which you get paid. So let's break it down....

In most cases you will get paid a fixed percentage of a sale. It could be as little as 3% (as it is with many Amazon products) or sometimes over 100% (which I know sounds crazy, but it's not a typo, so I'll explain more below.)

Depending on your target market and who you're an affiliate for, I see the range of 10%-50% commissions being pretty common. In fact, a lot of times the higher the cost of the product, the higher the commission. Like physical books (which typically range from $6-30) on Amazon are currently getting a 4.5% commission, and a digital course from Pat Flynn (which typically cost around $500) pays a 30% commission.

But some affiliate programs will pay a flat fee instead. My website hosting company I mentioned earlier, SiteGround, pays a flat $50 per paying referral. I've noticed this type of flat payment is also popular with monthly subscription boxes (like FabFitFun, that pays a flat $9 commission, and BarkBox pays $18.)

Other programs will pay you per click-through (typically a low number like five cents per click) or per lead (say a new newsletter subscriber or someone who has signed up for a free trial.)

A few programs I've seen will also pay a small fee for a lead, and then pay another commission on a sale if that same person ends up buying something.

To figure out how much money you might earn with a particular affiliate program, use the following formula:

First, you'll need to know your traffic numbers, and in regards to the program itself, you'll need to know the CTR (Click Through Rate), EPC (Earnings Per Click), AOV (Average Order Value), CR (Conversion Rate) and the RR (Reversal or Return Rate).

So let's imagine your site gets 20,000 visitors every month, and you're working with a company that pays you a 20% commission and the following are true:

CTR = 3%

AOV = $100

CR = 10%

RR = 10%

So we'd start with traffic:

Traffic = 20,000 x 3% CTR = 600

And then work out sales:

CTR 600 x 10% CR = 60 Sales

60 sales – RR 10% = 54 Sales

54 Sales x $100 AOV = $5400

$5400 x 20% commission = $1080 (earnings/commission)

And finally, to calculate your personal EPC, use the following formula:

EPC:

$1080 (Earnings) / 600 (Traffic) x 100 = $180

In many cases the affiliate program(s) you're working with will share their own EPC numbers. If they do, be sure to check your own against theirs to see how you're doing on average. Of course, you'll hope to be earning above average, but if you're not, you may have to tweak your campaign accordingly.

Two-Tier and Recurring Commissions

It's important to know about both two-tier and recurring payment programs, because these types of programs will leverage your income and make it more regular.

A two-tier affiliate program means that you get commissions on your referred affiliate's sales. For example, if you refer another blogger to a two-tier affiliate program, you can earn a (typically smaller) percentage of all of *their* sales, too.

This leverages your income because the people you've referred are also, in a way, helping you make more money. Of course, getting people to sign up for an affiliate program just to make money off of them is not what reputable businesses want. So the second tier of payments will be much lower.

For instance, MaxBounty (an affiliate network) pays a 5% commission of referred affiliate's earnings for the first 12 months. So if I refer another blogger to MaxBounty and they make $1000 per month in affiliate commissions, I also get $50 from those sales. It's not a lot, but it can add up and it's a nice little thank you for referring someone to them.

Recurring affiliate commissions are when you get paid over and over, as long as the person remains a customer of that company. (Or for a set period of time, like one year.)

A lot of SaaS (Software as a Service) companies pay this way. Like: ClickFunnels, ConvertKit, Tailwind, etc. It makes sense, because they charge monthly, whereas a one-time product purchase (like shoes from Nike) couldn't offer that same kind of recurring payment (unless they started a shoe of the month club. (Which would actually be a pretty good idea! *You're welcome*, Nike.)

In very few cases, some companies offer both two-tier **and** recurring payments. I call these the "unicorns" of affiliate marketing. They are rare, and magical! Because you can really start to see a more consistent income with them.

For more information about these "Unicorns" please visit my website at:

www.thrivingaffiliates.com/recommends/unicorn/

Chapter 2 - How to do Affiliate Marketing Legally AND Ethically

There are definitely some rules, both legal and ethical, that I want you to know about (and follow) right away. Some people will get scared off by this, but not you. I want you to feel empowered and to know you're doing all the right things when it comes to making money with affiliate marketing.

You may have heard the stories about Kendall Jenner getting sued by the F.T.C. because she wasn't disclosing the fact that she was being paid for certain Instagram posts. She could have avoided all that by simply adding "#ad" to her posts.

But it's not only influencers with millions of followers that have to follow the FTC's rules – we all do. I've included links to a few key areas on their website, because a). I'm not a lawyer and b). they actually explain it all in an easy to understand (and sometimes even humorous ways, like their blog post that says "Influencers, are your #materialconnection #disclosures #clearandconspicuous?" They also clearly address us as affiliate marketers (rather than, say paid endorsements). (Links in the references section and book bonuses.)

While I highly encourage you to read through those FTC links, in the meantime, essentially what they're asking is that you make your affiliate links "clear and conspicuous."

This means that if you have affiliate links in a blog post, disclose that fact. If I have more than one affiliate link in a post, I will add the disclosure right at the top of the page (you can always see how I do this on my blog at www.ThrivingAffiliates.com/blog). If there's only one affiliate link in a post, I'll mention it right around the link itself.

But there's a bit more to do, too. I have my short disclosure, but I also include some version of "click here for more information." That way, if someone doesn't understand what affiliate marketing even is, that link will pop open in a new tab with a more in-depth explanation of how affiliate marketing works, and also how I use it in an ethical way. I'm not trying to make sales just to make money, I'm recommending things I actually use and/or enjoy. If I haven't used them myself, I disclose that fact, too.

This is all on my "affiliate disclaimer" page, which is a vital part of every affiliate marketer's website. Be sure to add one to your own site, asap. You should never copy another person's affiliate disclaimer, but you can look at mine, or simply Google "affiliate disclaimer page examples" for inspiration and ideas for your own.

Other Places You Must Disclose Affiliate Links

Your website is not the only place you must disclose affiliate links. You must also disclose them in Instagram, Facebook, Twitter and any other social media posts. As well as in the description of any "pins" on Pinterest. And if you include affiliate links in your emails, those must be disclosed as well.

Basically, anywhere you place an affiliate link, you must "clearly and conspicuously" disclose them.

Some people are slightly confused by this, though. Say you post an image with a link on Pinterest that leads to a blog post that contains affiliate links. Do you have to disclose that in the pin description? No, because the link isn't going directly to an affiliate link, it's going to your blog post and you will have the disclosure there.

Of course, if you do pin an image on Pinterest that goes directly to an affiliate link, you must disclose it then. And that goes not just for Pinterest, but any place you're promoting your blog and/or your affiliate links directly.

Read the Rules

It should go without saying, but we live in a world where we quickly scroll through a terms and service agreement in seconds, barely giving it a look before clicking that "agree" button at the bottom of a page. Maybe, in some cases, you can do that. But NOT when you're joining an affiliate program.

Each affiliate program has their own rules and you want to be sure you're following them to the letter. Because they can (and will) kick you out.

For instance, as of the time I'm writing this, you

cannot use any Amazon affiliate links in emails (or PDFs, offline printed materials, and more!) That's a big no-no.

In another example: Etsy doesn't allow you to pin items directly on Pinterest. But guess what? They *used* to. Which brings up another point: if a program you're in sends you an email saying their rules and/or terms have changed, make sure you read and understand them.

At some point you'll probably see other people doing this stuff, but that doesn't mean it's okay.

The good news is, in most cases, you will be assigned an affiliate manager that you can go to with any questions or concerns you may have. If there is something you don't understand, reach out to them! I've found them very helpful. Afterall, the more successful *you* are, the more successful *they* are, too.

Affiliate Marketing Ethics

We've talked about the rules and laws associated with affiliate marketing, but I also want to talk about ethics.

You see, there is a lot of money to be made with affiliate marketing, which, unfortunately leads some people to do it in spammy, slimy, money-hungry ways.

Listen, I'm writing this book because I know and believe that you and I can both make a wonderful living with affiliate marketing. That could be an extra $100-1000 a month, or, $100,000 or more per month like bloggers Pat Flynn (of SmartPassiveIncome.com) or Michelle Schroeder-Gardner (of MakingSenseofCents.com).

I mention these two bloggers specifically because they are both *extremely* ethical when it comes to affiliate marketing. They always disclose links in their blogs, emails, social media, etc. You'll even hear Pat mention that a link he's suggesting is an affiliate link in his Podcast and YouTube videos. Never once have I seen him use an affiliate link and *not* disclose it.

THAT is the type of affiliate marketer I aspire to be, and I hope you do, too.

And it's not just about disclosure of the links themselves. It's about being honest about things like: if you've actually used the product or service or not. How much you actually liked your experience with it. Because let me tell you, there are some high-commission, low-quality products, services, courses, etc. for sale out there that just aren't worth the money. But some people will still endorse them, just to make that commission.

Please don't be that person.

The truth is: you don't have to be! There are so many high-quality products, services, courses, etc. for you to be an affiliate for that also pay well, you don't need to be anything *but* ethical.

I believe that most people will sense if you're being phony or smarmy, anyway, and won't buy through your links. So, in the long run, for your business and reputation, it's better to just be honest and ethical.

Chapter 3 – Is Affiliate Marketing Passive Income?

One thing people ask me all the time is, "Is affiliate marketing passive income?" And then they're annoyed when I say "Yes... *and* no."

But before I explain what I mean by that, let me just explain what passive income is, for those who might not yet know...

Everyone talks about passive income as in "making money while you sleep!" and how awesome it is.

The truth is, it *is* nice.

But you know what? I prefer to make money when I'm out on an adventure, or spending time with my family and friends, or art journaling, or even just relaxing on the couch. Making money while you sleep is fine, but making money while you're out *enjoying life* is even better!

I have an app on my phone that notifies me anytime one of my ebooks sell, and while that isn't affiliate marketing, I wanted to share this list I started of just some of the fun things I was doing when I received those notifications. Here are a few:

- While I was out having my birthday dinner with family and friends.
- While I was on vacation in California.
- While I was painting.
- While I was at a blogging conference.
- While I was picnicking with friends by the river.
- While I was doing karaoke with my daughter.
- While I was at an Etsy sellers' meet-up.
- While I was on an airplane.
- While I was at the movies.
- While I was at a mastermind meeting.
- While I was working.

- And, of course, while I was sleeping!

That's the really great thing about passive income: not that it happens while you're sleeping, but while you're out living a fuller, happier life!

But what is passive income, *really*? (Especially when it comes to online business and affiliate marketing.)

It's income you make from something you work on once (like a blog post, video, etc.), and can sell and/or promote over and over again, without having to make it again. Typically, this means more work up front (sometimes a little more, and sometimes a lot more.)

Some examples include:

- Affiliate Marketing via a blog post, product review, etc.
- Teaching a class on video that can be sold over and over.
- Creating online courses.
- Writing a book.
- Advertising on your blog.

What passive income is *not*:

Easy. You still have to work for it!

Quick. Passive income definitely does not happen overnight. It takes time to create blog posts, promote them, make them popular, and start getting sales. Your affiliate earnings might trickle in at first. (*Just don't give up!*)

Or even totally hands off. Because, just like with physical products or services, or different business models, you still have to promote what you've made. Which, with affiliate marketing, typically means getting people on your list, to your website, or following you in order to get them to click and buy things through your links.

But guess what else it isn't?

Impossible.

There are people making passive income on the internet every single day.

There are definitely other types of passive income, like:

- Real Estate, Investing
- Stocks and Bonds
- Royalties (books, music, etc.)
- Businesses you may own but don't actively participate in
- Trust funds
- Portfolio Income
- Licensing
- Billboards
- Rent out things you're not using (cars, RVs, boats, etc.)
- Etc.

Along with affiliate marketing, all of these forms of passive income have some form of "action" needed.

So is Affiliate Marketing Passive or Not?

After reading through the description of affiliate marketing above, you can probably see why I say yes *and* no to that question.

I say yes because I can show you countless examples

of people who wrote one blog post that makes them thousands of dollars each year (or month!) over and over again, even after they haven't touched it in years. (Myself included!)

If that's not passive income, I don't know what is!? It's just like authors who wrote a book and continue to get royalties from it for years, or even decades later. Or songwriters who wrote a hit and earn ongoing royalties.

But affiliate marketing is also *not* passive income at times.

Here are some examples why and/ or how:

Some online business owners who have affiliate programs for their online courses only launch those courses once per year. If you're an affiliate for them, you're likely to do one big push for their products once per year, too. You might send emails, do Facebook and/or Instagram Lives, you might do webinars, you might even create a bonus for those people who purchase through your affiliate link!

And once the business owner who has the affiliate program closes their carts, you're done. You've made all the referrals you could have, and you'll receive one (hopefully) big commission check about 60 days later (to account for refunds, etc.)

That's not passive at all. That's a whole lot of work, in fact! BUT, it's also just *one* way to do affiliate marketing, and you don't have to if you don't want to.

But even with a simple blog post containing affiliate links, you may need to go back and update it from time to time. Maybe the products you linked to are no longer available. Or the course you've linked to has been completely updated and changed. Or the software you're promoting has been upgraded so your post will need to be updated with the changes, too.

Plus I'm always writing new blog posts with more (or different) affiliate links in them. So while I may still be earning affiliate income from a post I wrote two years ago, I'm actively working on new posts I hope will also pay me for years to come.

If I stopped writing new posts (etc.) and/or promoting my old posts today, I'd still earn income month after month. But truthfully, that income will most likely go down and down, until it completely dwindles away.

What I like is the fact that, while I started my

business working 40+ hours a week, the longer I work on it, the fewer hours I have to work every day. I don't set an alarm, and I have a 1-2 hour morning routine I do before I even start work. And because my husband gets off of work at 2:30, I generally stop for the day around that same time, usually only working for 5 hours or so. And my goal is to work 2-3 hours per day, eventually.

And I know that will be possible because of the (largely) passive income I earn with affiliate marketing.

Chapter 4 - Choosing a Niche

Unless you already have a blog and a niche, this chapter will help you decide what you actually want to blog about, how you will incorporate affiliate marketing, and how to get started.

No matter how you say it (rhymes with bee-sh or rhymes with rich), you're going to have to choose a niche.

So what is a niche, anyway? A niche (in regards to online business and blogging) is basically the topic you'll cover that focuses in on a smaller population of people.

But wait, why would you want to target a *smaller* population of people? Because, believe it or not, it's actually easier to make money if you do! I started out by trying to help creatives and bloggers and online business owners (and anyone who would listen, really!) how to build a successful online business that would help them create lives the love.

That sounds great, right? Well, it was... for a little while. Until I realized that it was just too broad of a subject, and I couldn't teach about every aspect of online business to every different type of online business owner!

So, after way too long (honestly) I finally found my niche: teaching bloggers and online business owners how to monetize their blogs and make money online with affiliate marketing.

I was no longer teaching about social media or Facebook ads or work-at-home jobs or accountability partners, etc., etc. I'm now teaching affiliate marketing exclusively.

Let's come up with some examples of this, to help you figure out *your* own niche. But let's start by covering some popular blogging topics:

- fashion

- parenthood

- business

- lifestyle

- personal finance

- travel

- health and fitness

- beauty

- home / interior design

- blogging

- food

- relationships/dating

- weddings

- DIY

Now let's see some ways we could niche down on these topics:

- A fashion blog could be exclusively about: shoes for women over 40, minimal jewelry, plus size clothing, sustainable clothes, handmade fashion, high fashion toddlers, comfortable clothes, office attire, etc.

- A parenthood blog could be about: being a single

parent, co-parenting, for parents who want to work at home, parenting interracial children, parenting twins, parenting toddlers, parenting teenagers, or even a blog about transitioning when children move out, a.k.a "empty nesters", etc.

• Business blogs could be anything from: marketing tips, teaching people how to sell on Etsy, all about social media marketing, email marketing, copywriting, women-owned businesses, course creating, business coaching, side hustles, work-at-home job opportunities, selling on Amazon, passive income, etc.

• Lifestyle blogs tend to be broader, so you might talk about a variety of subjects from the list, but also niche down. Like: living in Los Angeles, or living on a budget, or living minimally, or living off the grid, etc.

• Personal finance bloggers could write about things like: paying off debt, frugality, investing, saving money, money when you're married, buying a house, how to improve your credit, quickly paying off student loans, managing credit card debt, etc.

• Travel bloggers obviously blog about travel, but

you could get very specific and blog about traveling in an RV, by boat, etc., or traveling in a certain country or region, traveling with kids, traveling alone, city travel guides, in-depth travel guides about the city (or state) you live in, etc.

- Health and fitness bloggers can blog about: exercising over 50, yoga for plus size people, healthy eating for families, essential oils, workouts for baseball players, eating for bodybuilders, fun ways to get kids to exercise, etc.

- Beauty blog subjects can range from makeup to hair to skincare, or get even more specific and blog about: makeup for women of color, haircare and styling for curly hair, avant-garde makeup ideas, retro inspired makeup ideas, etc.

- Home and interior design blogs could be about: home makeovers, design on a budget, modern/country/coastal/etc. décor, choosing art for the home, or zero in on kids' rooms, finished basements, craft rooms, bathrooms, lofts, etc.

- Yes, there are blogs about blogging... in fact, I do a bit of blogging about blogging on my blogs, too. But you could niche down and blog about beauty blogging, lifestyle blogging, mom blogs, etc.

- Relationship/dating bloggers could blog about dating in the big city (or small towns), long distance relationships, same sex relationships, date night ideas, improving your marriage, etc.

- Food blogs can be as expansive or as niche as you can imagine: there is one blog exclusively talking about Amish Friendship Bread! That's it. ONE subject. And they're killing it. But yours could be about appetizers, brunch, desserts, or types of eating like Paleo, low calorie, Keto, alkaline, etc. Or what about foods kids will love that are healthy, or feeding large families on a budget, etc.

- Wedding niches include topics like destination weddings, DIY weddings, wedding dresses, wedding decor, different styles of weddings, unique wedding ideas, and more.

- DIY blogs are so much fun and could include ideas like, Home DIYs, DIYs for kids, modern DIYs, quick (under 5 minutes, under an hour, etc.) DIY projects, colorful DIY projects, dollar store DIYs, DIYs for teens, etc.

I could go on and on, because these ideas are really just the tip of the iceberg!

Plus, there are blogs about: sports (of all kinds), video games/gaming, pop culture, humor, music, cosplay, web design, dance, electronics, toys, writing, work-at-home jobs, minimalism, personal development, vacuums (yes, really!), outdoor activities, aging parents, spirituality, tarot, quotes, movies, green living, tiny houses, RVing, outer space, filmmaking, books/book clubs, knitting, creativity, planners, art journals, geology, review sites, and on and on...

Pretty much any subject you can imagine, *there's a blog about it*. But don't let that deter you. In fact, it should *excite* you! Because if someone is already successfully blogging about a subject you want to blog about, you know there's already interest in it and it's time to bring **your** voice to the table.

There are a couple of schools of thought on choosing a topic or niche for your blog.

The first is to choose something you're passionate about. Because blogging *does* become a business --

therefore something you'll be spending 20-40 hours a week doing. With that in mind, blogging about something you're passionate about makes sense! You might as well do something you enjoy every day, right?

Well, some people say no. They say that you should start a blog based on its ability to make money. Because your passions may not pay the bills.

I kind of agree/disagree with both. While finding a topic you love is important (at least to me -- I believe in doing what you love for a living!) you also need to make money with it. Unless you don't need it to make money and just want to do it as a hobby... That's fine, too!

But I'm guessing since you've read this far, you want to make money with your blog and affiliate marketing. So finding a topic that you love *and* one that can make money are pretty much equally important, if you ask me.

But you'll have to decide for yourself, or course.

The cool thing is, there is an affiliate program for just about every niche you can imagine, so your chances of choosing something to blog about that you can make profitable are pretty good!

If you're thinking, *"Well, I don't really want to start a*

blog!" Don't worry. I'll get to that in a future chapter. Because, while having a blog can make affiliate marketing easier, it's actually not required!

Choose a Niche

Some people may read through the list of ideas I mention in this chapter and feel totally inspired! They'll know right away what they want to do and get to it.

On the other hand, some people may look at it and feel totally overwhelmed. Maybe they have too many ideas and can't choose just one. Or maybe it's just so many they can't even think about what they would pick at all.

If that's you, I understand. Quite frankly, I'm in the first boat – I see an idea and I want to start working on it right away! Of course, this can backfire, too. Because I'm multi-passionate and I know how to start a business online, I've started (and stopped and/or sold) more blogs than I care to admit!

But I've met many other would-be online business owners who, despite having a bunch of ideas presented to them (or maybe because there are so many ideas in front of them), they still can't choose one.

If that's you, first, I want you to consider something: Most entrepreneurs don't end where they start. By that I mean you will likely go on a journey with your business.

For instance, I started out years ago doing web design. Then I had an "online magazine" about having a home-based business (it was essentially a blog before they were invented). I wrote a couple of ebooks that were bestsellers (again, before Kindle was a thing). I sold art and refurbished furniture on eBay. I sold vintage items on Etsy. I created and sold niches sites. I was an Instagram influencer. I had another blog about being your own boss. And now I have ThrivingAffiliates.com where I teach exclusively about affiliate marketing.

Talk about a journey! Mind you, this was all over the last 20 years or so.

So if you choose to start a blog about being a single parent, and in 3 years you get married again, it's okay. You can sell that blog or transition it to a blog about being in a blended family, or you can start something completely different.

When you choose a niche, you're definitely not stuck in it.

On the flipside: if you don't see success right away (but you still like your niche and/or see its potential), stick with it! That is one mistake I've not only made myself, but have seen far too many others make. They quit... probably right before things start to get good, too.

I would say, if you're starting from scratch, you should be prepared to make very little money your first 6-12 months. Some people can start earning much sooner, and others will never quite figure out how to make a living with affiliate marketing. But from what I've seen, I believe 6-12 months is a realistic timeline.

Of course, if you start a blog, there are other ways to make money with it, like offering a service, or creating a course, or selling a product, etc. Those may provide some income in the meantime, if you're in a rush to make a full-time living with your blog right away.

But again, the reason I love affiliate marketing so much (compared to those other ways of making money) is because of how passive it is. Yes, it may take some time and effort in the beginning, but it can also earn you income for years to come (whereas a service or being a coach, etc., will only pay you for the exact hours you put into it.)

Once you've chosen your niche, it's time to take the next step.

Choose a Domain

A domain name, in case you don't know, is the website address, or URL for your blog and/or website. For instance, my domain name is ThrivingAffiliates.com

You can choose a domain name based on your topic or niche, your business name, your actual name, or just a made up word or words, if you'd like.

I personally like domain names to give me a clue as to what I'm going to find on the site. But if you created a cute name for your toddler fashion blog, well that's okay, too.

As I mentioned, my blog ends with ".com" and I highly recommend you get a domain that ends with .com, too. There are hundreds of other choices these days (like .co, .biz, .art, .shop, etc.) But people are so used to typing in .com at the end of a domain, that if you don't get one, you might just be missing out.

I like to buy my domains from NameCheap.com because they're not only inexpensive (as the name implies

– under $10 in most cases) but they also offer free "WhoIsGuard" (as of the time I'm writing this) which is awesome because it essentially protects your name, phone number, mailing address and email address from being added to a bunch of spam lists.

I once registered a domain once without it, and within 48 hours I got nearly twenty phone calls from people offering web design services. It was so annoying. And that was just the start!

So no matter where you register your domain, be sure to opt for the privacy option (whether you have to pay for it or not.)

Ideally, you'll want your domain name and social media handles to be the same. If you have a long domain name, try to shorten your social media handles in all the same way.

For example, say your domain was something like BringingUpDaisies.com.

Well, BringingUpDaisies is too long for sites like Twitter (who only allow 15 characters for your @name) so you'd have to shorten it. (I had to shorten my Twitter handle to @ThrivingsAffs.) Pinterest and Instagram allow up to 30 letters/characters, and Facebook allows 75 characters for a Page name. So you might want to shorten it to something like BUpDaisies for social media, across all accounts to make it cohesive and easy to share.

Or, if Twitter isn't important to you at all (which is a reasonable idea) then keep the full name across all the sites you'll *actually* be on.

But say you're lucky enough to get a short domain name, like pinky.com (that was the first random word that came to my mind.) Next, you'll want to check to see if @pinky is available on social media sites you plan to use. If not, in that case, you may need to actually lengthen it. Maybe something like @therealpinky, @pinkyinc, etc. But before you buy your domain name, just be sure to check the social media handle availability and come up with a plan for what you'll do in case your name is taken.

I suggest having several domain ideas (either on paper or in a document on your phone or computer) and then start your search to see if they're available at NameCheap.com.

Again, ideally, you'll want a domain ending in dot com (because it's the most common and easiest to remember). But if your heart is set on a certain name, and it's only available with a different extension, it doesn't have to be the end of the world. You can just work with what you get and make the best of it!

Get Started!

Once you've chosen a domain, you'll want to get started right away! Creating a website is a book in itself, but I've included a handy link to starting a blog that makes passive income with affiliate marketing in the free book bonus mentioned at the beginning of this book.

But in general this includes things like: creating your website, getting a logo (you can get one made for $5 on Fiverr.com or check out Etsy for more options), or make one yourself (Canva.com makes it really easy!), and signing up for any/all social media sites you plan on using. Right now I recommend at least signing up for Pinterest (for sure!), and Instagram and a Facebook business Page, at the minimum.

Once you've created a few blog posts (I recommend 5 to 10 to start, but the more, the better), plus your "about", "privacy policy", "affiliate disclosure", "terms and conditions" and "contact" pages, you can start applying to affiliate programs that fit your niche. How exciting!

I suggest having the pages listed above, as well as several blog posts before you apply to affiliate programs because many will look at your site before they approve you. Even with that bare minimum site up, you still may not be approved. But don't worry! I'll go over what to do if that happens in a future chapter. But for now, just be aware that, in most cases, you're truly "applying" to be an affiliate; so you want to put your very best effort into each application.

Chapter 5 - Finding Affiliate Programs to Apply to

By now you either have an existing blog you want to add affiliate links to, or you've just created one. Congrats! You're about to embark on an exciting money-making journey.

You're first (or next) step is to find affiliate programs to join. This can be fun or frustrating. Let's make it as fun as possible!

When you're just starting out, Amazon's affiliate program is a good one to join. As of this writing, you will pretty much automatically be approved, so that's a win right away. And because Amazon sells just about everything under the sun (from books to houses – yes, you can buy a tiny house on Amazon!) you're very likely to find something you can recommend and/or review for your readers.

The thing is, in order to *stay on* as an Amazon affiliate you will need to make a sale within your first 180 days. (So if you don't have a blog up and running yet; don't apply to Amazon until you do in order to give yourself the best chance of making a sale in that time.)

Don't think you can game the system, either. Amazon somehow knows if your sale came from a friend or family member, and that is a no-no that can potentially get your affiliate account banned.

Just create the most amazing blog post(s) you can and promote it (/them) like crazy once you've joined Amazon.

Also note that you cannot use Amazon link in emails, and you cannot "grab" images from Amazon to use in your blog post (unless you're using an approved plugin like AMZImage). I'll share more "don'ts" in a later chapter, too.

But where might you find other affiliate programs to join?

The first place to look is where you actually shop. If you're blogging about fashion, you might want to check out sites that sell clothes you want to blog about. Maybe that's

Nordstrom, or maybe that's Old Navy, etc. Go to their site(s), scroll all the way down to the bottom on the first page and look for something like:

- Affiliate program
- Referral Partners
- Publishers
- Become an affiliate
- Etc.

Usually if they have an affiliate program, they will have a link for it there. But there are cases where you'll have to dig a little deeper. If you don't find any helpful information in the footer, try a simple Google search. Something like: "Nordstrom affiliate program".

If the company you're searching for does have an affiliate program, it's likely to come up on the first page of Google.

If they don't, that's not always the end of the world (or the end of your search!) If your blog and/or following is large and targeted, you can also simply reach out to the company you'd like to be an affiliate for, and see if they would be interested in partnering up.

They won't always say yes, of course. But those who do will likely be very excited to have you as an affiliate, seeing as you sought them out as a perfect partner for your following.

Affiliate Networks

I discussed Affiliate Networks a bit in chapter one, so you should be aware of what they are and in general how they work.

Networks are a great way to find a bunch of affiliate programs in your niche at one time. For example, if you join the ShareASale network, you can simply log in and click on Merchant Search and you'll see they have over 4500 merchants to choose from.

Now, 4500 may feel overwhelming, but they categorize the merchants by type. So if you have a gardening blog, you can simply search within the Home & Garden section. Right now there are over 700 merchants in that section, but you can click on it and do another search to narrow your results even further.

Searching "organic gardening" reduces your

merchant results to under 40 – a much more manageable number. From there you can check out the companies / programs that look interesting to you and decide from there whether or not you'd like to apply.

All the networks work in a similar fashion, and I've included links to some of my favorites and most popular in the book bonus download.

Commissions Are Not (Always) Set in Stone

When you do research and/or sign up for different affiliate programs, they will tell you their terms: cookie length, commission percentage, commission type (recurring, flat fee, etc.), etc.

If you already have a large blog readership, email list, and/or social media following, it's possible to negotiate a higher affiliate commission with some companies.

If you try this with Amazon, you might get laughed off of the Internet. But some small to mid-size companies will be open to this idea. And why not!? If you can bring them a bunch of new customers, many will be more than happy to work with you.

Some will give you higher commissions, some will

even offer your readers a special discount or a deal exclusive to you and your affiliate links. Some will do both!

I always say, the answer to an un-asked question is always no, so you might as well at least try for the yes.

I know one blogger who knows her audience so well she can gauge about how much she will sell with any product or service she recommends. If a company is only offering a 10% commission, she knows it won't be worth her time to create a blog post, when another company selling similar products or services might offer 25% or more.

In that case, she will approach company A and mention that she would like to work with them (over company B) and why she believes her post will be worth a higher commission. She also has a media kit and explains that she'll not only share it on her blog, but on social media, to her email list, and on her podcast, as well.

In a case like that, who would say no? (According to her, most of the time she gets a yes.)

Now I realize you may be just starting out and that her big numbers don't apply to you. But you never know... Sometimes having a tight niche, even with "beginner" numbers – along with a positive attitude – will help you get higher commissions.

But another way to get higher commissions is by referring a lot of customers. Once you've done that, you can always go in and re-negotiate more money. Again, you won't always get a positive response, but it can't hurt and only help to ask.

What if Your Application is Rejected?

What if you apply to a program and you get a rejection? Well, first take a deep breath and know this happens to all of us.

I created an amazing niche site I was soooo excited about and it was largely (like 90%) based on a certain program I wanted to promote. So I created the site, signed up for all the social media, wrote a dozen (awesome – if I do say so myself) blog posts. And I finally applied to the affiliate program for that company and I was immediately rejected.

I thought: *Well, they must not have seen my website? Or maybe they're just not taking affiliates on right now. That's it… I'll try again in a couple of weeks!*

So I wrote more awesome posts, and applied again a few weeks later. Again: instant rejection.

This time I took a more proactive approach (and this is one of the things I recommend you do if your blog has been rejected for some reason or another) and I found the contact information for the affiliate manager and I sent them a very polite email asking why I was rejected, and how I could possibly change my website in order to be approved.

I waited for a reply... and waited and waited. I didn't hear back so I sent a follow up email a couple of weeks later.

Still, nothing.

And because the site I created was so heavily focused on that one company's program, after several more weeks I realized I had to shut it down.

The good news is, I learned something very important when this happened. First, you don't want even 50% of your affiliate earnings coming from one place, because if that company makes changes, or you accidentally break the terms of service and they kick you out, or they just stop their affiliate program all together...

Well, you're now out 50% (or more!) of our monthly income. Not fun. Not at all.

But I have a close friend who signed up for the Etsy affiliate program and when she first applied her blog was rejected. She was determined to get into their affiliate program, however, and reached out to the affiliate manager to see why her blog had been rejected.

In her case, the blog was simply too new: there wasn't enough content there – yet! – in order for Etsy to confidently say yes to her application. So my friend kept working on her blog, adding new posts, making sure her affiliate disclaimer page was up to par, etc.

Several weeks later she applied again, and was approved!

So it's not always a sad story like mine.

The point is, if you do get rejected and it means a lot to you to work with that specific brand or company, reach out to them and (very politely) ask why, and what you may be able to do to turn that no into a yes.

How to Avoid Getting Rejected in the First Place

If you're a new blogger, it will be harder to get

approved by some affiliate programs. But there is one "trick" (which is not really a trick at all) that I have seen help new bloggers get approved for affiliate programs they might have been rejected for otherwise.

That is to simply make THE BEST blog post you can featuring that product or service, but without affiliate links.

For instance, you could create an in-depth review post of a product or service you absolutely love. Be fair in the post, and mention any improvements you'd like to see, along with praise for what you *do* love about it. Make sure everything is as close to perfect as possible, including images, the written words, etc. Then work on getting people to share that post, so it shows up in your social share numbers.

Once you've done that, then contact the affiliate manager before you even apply and let them know that you have this very popular post on your blog about their product or service, and that you'd like to be an affiliate for them. Mention that you'll be applying as soon as possible, asking them if there is anything else you can possibly do in order to get your application approved.

I can't say this will work 100% of the time, but every

time I've seen someone do it, it has worked. So if you really, really want to get approved for a certain product or service, you can certainly try this technique.

As an alternative, let's say you're a vegan food blogger and there is one type of vegan soup base that you use all the time. In fact, you've mentioned it in fifteen different recipes. That's another way to show a certain company that you're a huge fan and you'd make a great affiliate for them.

Just like you want to be an honest and ethical affiliate for your readers, you also want to be friendly and easy to worth with when dealing with affiliate managers. It will go a long way with your overall success.

Chapter 6 - Affiliate Marketing with a Blog

Most people are going to do affiliate marketing with a blog, so I'll start here. There are so many ways you can incorporate affiliate marketing on your blog, but I'd actually like to start out with the easiest way – if you already have a blog. (Next up I'll share ideas on how and where to immediately incorporate affiliate links when you're just starting your blog.)

If you already have a blog and you haven't used any (or many) affiliate links, the first thing you want to do is log into Google analytics and find your top fifteen most popular posts. Then go through each post, one by one, to see how and where you might be able to add affiliate links.

Because you're just starting out, you may need to take notes and find specific affiliate programs that will work for your posts. In that case, go through the top three to start, and then go start finding and applying to the related affiliate programs. While you wait to get approved for those, go through the next three and do the same thing. Rinse and repeat this process until you've gone through your top fifteen posts.

In most cases, this will be pretty easy! If you're a paleo food blogger and one of your most popular posts is "10 Paleo Snacks That Actually Taste Great" you can simply link to any of those snacks that are sold on Amazon and/or elsewhere.

But say you're a mommy blogger and your most popular post is about traveling with toddlers. Depending on what you've written about, you could include affiliate links for things like; deals on travel, the luggage you used to fit everything you needed to bring – without it being too heavy or cumbersome, the books or toys you brought to entertain the kinds on long flights, drives, or train rides, the perfect lightweight blanket that will keep them warm without taking up too much space in your carry-on, etc.

They key is, just be creative!

And while you may only have one link to any given

product, deal, course, or service throughout your post, you can also include a handy checklist at the end of the post with everything (or at the very least, the "highlights") you've recommended throughout the post.

Surprising Places to Put Affiliate Links

Whether you're starting a blog from scratch or you've already been blogging for months or years, there are a few places on your blog that you may not have considered adding affiliate links (and if you haven't, you're missing out!)

Your Resources Page.

The first page every blog should have, filled with affiliate links of course, is a Resources page. Resources will vary from blog to blog, but let's cover some general blog types, and how they might use this page.

Travel Blog Resource Page Ideas

Travel bloggers might have a resources page that includes a list of items you don't want to forget on your trip. And/or a list of "deal" travel sites. And/or a list of luggage for X types of travelers: parents, backpackers, minimalists, adventure seekers, retirees, etc.

Food Blog Resource Page Ideas

Food bloggers might have a resources page that includes a list of items every kitchen should have. Or your favorite places to get hard-to-find ingredients. Or a list of every pan for the job (and list your favorite pans for baking, making eggs, boiling pasta, etc.) Or your top ten favorite cookbooks, etc.

Business Blog Resource Page Ideas

Business bloggers might include affiliate links on their resources page that lists the top ten online courses for bloggers. Or the 3 online courses that will help you hit six figures. Or the books every business coach should read, etc.

Parenting Blog Resource Page Ideas

Parenting bloggers can include such a wide variety of affiliate links on their resource pages! Like your favorite books for naptime. Or the parenting books you couldn't have survived the teen years without. Or online parenting classes every mom of twins should take.

Relationship Blog Resource Page Ideas

If you're a relationship blogger, you might include affiliate links for low cost date night ideas (and drop in some Groupon links). Or gifts to give your significant other to show how much you appreciate them. Or the top ten things you might forget at your wedding. Or resources for shy daters, etc.

If your blog niche is not listed here and you can't think or what kind of resources you might list on your blog, hit me up on Instagram @ThrivingAffiliates and let me know what type of blog you have, and we can brainstorm some ideas together! (Yes, *really!*)

A Tools Page

Similar to a resources page, a tool's page simply lists things you use and recommend, for whatever niche it is you're serving. For instance, I have an "Affiliate Marketing Tools" page where I share some of the tools that help me make more money with affiliate marketing, and I believe they can help other affiliate marketers make more money, too.

In my case, the tools range from website hosting, to an email service provider, to content writers, web design tools, growth tools, automation tools, etc. The tools I list will be helpful to all affiliate marketers, not just to people who blog about affiliate marketing.

So what kind of tools might your readers need? Again, let's look at different types of blogs and come up with several ideas for each:

Fashion Blog Tools Page Ideas

Some tools fashion bloggers might list: The best shopping deals of the year (with a list of sales that big stores have coming up). The things I use to keep my closet organized. The fashion magazines that never go out of style. (And yes, you can use Amazon affiliate links for magazine subscriptions!)

Lifestyle Blog Tools Page Ideas

Lifestyle bloggers might have a tools list that includes ten things they just couldn't live without. Lifehacks they wished they'd known sooner. A list of tools every single person should own before age 25. Etc.

Personal Finance Tools Page Ideas

Personal finance bloggers could make a tools list of the top ways to reduce credit card debt. A list of sites that will help you save more money. Or the best books on finance for newlyweds. Tools for saving for early retirement, etc.

Health and Fitness Blog Tools Page Ideas

Health and Fitness bloggers could list: the home gym equipment every fitness geek should own. Or the best workout DVDs for people who hate the gym. Or the tools I use in the kitchen that help me cut calories. Etc.

Beauty Blog Tools Page Ideas

Beauty bloggers could list their favorite make-up application tools. Or their go to beauty products. Or the 5 things every woman should carry in her purse. The tools I use to tame my curly hair, etc.

Blogging About Blogging Tools Page Ideas

Bloggers who blog about blogging could share their top favorite software tools that make blogging easier. Or a list of tools that will help with blog performance, etc.

DIY Blog Tools Page Ideas

DIY bloggers could include a list of crafting tools that every DIYer should have on hand. Or a list of their favorite DIY kits that come with the tools and supplies included, etc.

Other Pages You Can Include Affiliate Links

Similar to the tools and/or resources pages, you could also include a _your name or blog name_ recommends... page. This could include all kinds of things, depending on your niche.

Some examples include: books, courses, software, tools, wardrobe staples, freebies, ebooks, webinars, certain brand items that pertain to your niche, etc.

For people new to your site and/or whatever it is you're blogging about, you could also have a "start here" page where you list the things a beginner might need to have on hand.

One genius way to include affiliate links on a page is like how Thomas Frank of College Info Geek shares a packing list for new college students. (You can see that at https://collegeinfogeek.com/college-packing-list/). Of course, you'll have to figure out what your "packing list" is for your niche and readers. But don't hesitate to get creative!

Those are some pages you can create on your blog to generate addition affiliate income. Now let's talk about blog posts.

Affiliate Specific vs. Topic Specific

There are many ways to create blog posts that include affiliate links, and I'll cover most, if not all in this chapter. For now let's talk about affiliate specific posts versus topic affiliate posts.

An affiliate specific post is one you write that is all about that particular affiliate's product or products.

An example of this might be a review of a particular course. You would go in-depth about the course, explaining what you liked and didn't like about it, etc.

In that case, it doesn't make sense to include affiliate

links for a bunch of other stuff. Maybe a link for a competing course (especially if you've reviewed that course as well. But then you'd simply send them to the other review, not directly to the affiliate link, anyway.)

An affiliate specific post will go in deep one way or another (more ideas about this in Chapter 12.)

A topic specific post goes in-depth on a certain topic, and will likely include affiliate links from a variety of places.

One example of this would be a fashion bloggers outfit post. The jeans might be from Old Navy, the sweater from Target, the boots from Nordstrom Rack, the purse from Macy's, the jewelry from Etsy, and the top from T.J.Maxx.

Another example is a food blogger, writing a recipe post. You could link the food to Amazon affiliate link, but you could even use a Target link for the bowls you use, and a Lowe's link for the oven you're cooking in, etc.

It's good to have both of these types of blog posts on your blog. It's definitely a great way to create more affiliate links and create income streams from a variety of affiliate programs.

More Affiliate Blog Post Ideas

Below I'll share some more general blog post ideas. While they may seem general, it's by using these general ideas that you can create blog post after blog post, with a different, creative spin on each one.

- **Round ups**

Round ups are super fun and fairly quick and easy to create. Some ideas include: a food blogger round up of "game day appetizers" or "vegan friendly Thanksgiving dishes." A DIY blogger could write "10 Fun DIYs to do with Kids" or "Home Décor Projects You Can Finish in a Weekend." A travel blogger could write about "Fall Travel Deals You Don't Want to Miss" or "The best places to visit in January."

- **Gift Guides**

You might think gift guides won't fit your niche, but I challenge you to find a way to incorporate them! As a business blogger, I created a "Gift Guide for Boss Moms", so I know you can come up with something in *your* niche.

Let's brainstorm! A fitness blogger could write "10 Gifts to Buy Your BFF who Recently Lost Weight" (or bulked up, for that matter!) A food blogger could write "10 Best Gifts for New Bakers." A mom blog could create a list like "10 Gifts You Should NEVER Give New Parents, (And 10 They'll Thank You Forever For!)" A beauty blogger could write "10 Makeup Essentials Your Best Friend will LOVE for her Birthday."

- **Travel guides**

Obviously, travel guides won't be appropriate for every blogger, but they're not just for travel bloggers, either! A parenting blog could write, "15 things to do with kids in Such-in-such City." A lifestyle blogger could write about their favorite restaurants in the city they live in. A fitness blogger could share "The best places to work out when visiting New York." A blog about dating could write about "The Most Romantic Places to Share Your First Kiss in X City." If you blog about business and/or blogging, your post topic could be something like "Best Places to Work Remotely."

- **Must have lists**

Every blogger can come up with a must-have list – if not several! Because no matter what your niche, there are things people "must have".

Some quick ideas in different niches include:

Must have jackets for winter... Must have plugins for bloggers... Must have keto cookbooks... Must have workout equipment for your home gym... Must have supplies for a backpacking trip... 3 colors of lipstick every woman must have in her purse..., etc.

- **How to's**

How to posts are not just for DIY or food bloggers! I can think of all kinds of ideas for different niches, like:

- How to tie a tie
- How to teach your kids to ride a bike
- How to travel with just one carry on
- How to live mortgage free
- How to promote your art on Instagram
- How to write a book
- How to start selling your products on Amazon
- How to create an Etsy listing that sells

- How to quit sugar
- How to pay off student loans quickly
- How to create the perfect destination wedding
- How to break up and *actually* stay friends
- Etc.

- **Interviews**

Again, you might find it hard to come up with interview ideas, but I find them to be some of the best and easiest posts to create. They can be done via email, or by phone call and then transcribed.

Here are some ideas for different niches:
- Interview the teacher of a course you're promoting
- Interview the creator of a software product you endorse
- Interview an artist (and show their art with affiliate links)
- Interview a cookbook author
- Interview a jewelry designer (and link to their jewelry with affiliate links.)

- **Example posts**

Example posts might sound vague, so let me explain simply by sharing some, well, examples!

- Wedding Vows Examples
- Eye shadow types (matte, shimmer, glitter, etc.)
- Examples of luggage for families
- Examples of home gym equipment under $50 and how to use them
- Paint examples (watercolor vs. oil vs. acrylic vs. gouache, etc.)
- Examples of gluten-free flours

- **Feature posts**

Feature posts, in my examples, are kind of like the round-up post and interview post got together and had a baby. In this type of feature post you typically interview one person, and highlight whatever it is they make and sell. I like the idea especially for people who sell on Etsy (artists, makers, designers, etc.)

But you could also, for instance, feature several newlyweds, asking them what was the best thing about the décor at their weddings (and feature the décor items with affiliate links). Or ask several new parents what one item they couldn't live without and why (and feature those items with affiliate links). Ask other travel bloggers their favorite destinations (and include affiliate links for flights and/or hotels in those places).

My hope is that these lists of pages and post ideas has filled you with limitless things to blog about! I like to keep a running list of blog post ideas. I use Dynalist.io (because it has desktop and phone-based apps that sync up, so no matter where I am when I add the idea, the master list is updated.) But you could use a Word Doc, Google Docs, Evernote, or even a paper journal if that's what works best for you.

A couple of things I want you to remember when you're creating your blog posts (and I'll share even more in the SEO chapter), but be sure that images you include in your blog post are linked with your affiliate link to the product in the photo. People will/do click on photos all the time, so this is a great way for them to click on your affiliate links.

Also, if you can create buttons (Elementor is a free WordPress plugin that will allow you to make buttons in mere minutes!) use those buttons for some affiliate links, as well. I'm not sure what it is (or even if this is proven), but in my experience, people love to click on buttons! So use them, when and where appropriate, in your affiliate posts.

But the blog posts and pages aren't the only way you'll make money with affiliate marketing on your blog.

Social Media

I'm going to mention Social media (and by that I mean sites/apps like: Facebook, Instagram, Twitter, etc.) because some affiliate marketers are rocking it on social media.

I personally find my time is best spent on SEO for Google search and Pinterest, because those two sites bring me about 96% of my traffic.

But I also spent a long time organically building up

my Instagram account to around 100k followers... only to have IG all but lock down my engagement overnight. So I felt kind of burned by that and haven't personally spent a lot of time trying to promote on social media.

At the same time, I suggest you at least sign up for the accounts on today's most popular platforms. That way you can, at the very least, "reserve" your blog's name as your username, and you'll have it/them in case you want to start using them in the future.

I recommend you start using and building one social media platform at a time, in order to give yourself a chance to get to know how the platform itself works, and how you might monetize it with affiliate links.

Start with either: the platform *you* enjoy most or the platform your *ideal customers* are on the most. Once you've got a good grip on that first one, start the other one that you didn't choose to begin with.

Eventually, you might want to be everywhere on all the most popular social media platforms) or use one or two, mostly for fun to allow your readers to get to know you a bit more (so your time can be better spent elsewhere).

But unless or until you can see that social media directly affects your bottom line, I wouldn't worry about it too much at this point.

Just a note, YouTube and Pinterest are not social media sites, despite the fact that many people label them that way. They're actually search engines, like Google. Only Pinterest is a visual search engine and YouTube is a search engine for videos. I have a full chapter on doing affiliate marketing on Pinterest, and it's a good one! So watch out for that.

Build an Email List

One thing I do recommend you start doing right away is build an email list if you haven't already. You can even do this before you have a website! If you don't have a website yet, you can start building your email list with a "coming soon" page that lets visitors know that they can get on your list to be the first to know when your site goes live.

When it comes to building an email list, Pat Flynn (of SmartPassiveIncome.com) said:

"Looking back at the first business I created back in 2008, not having an email list was like shooting myself in the foot. It was

a huge mistake, because I sold products, but had no way of letting people—interested people —know that they existed. Even here, on Smart Passive Income, I didn't collect my first email address until 1.5 years after I started the blog. Big mistake—and I made it twice!"

Even though I'm touching on email list building in this chapter, I want to recommend Pat's tutorial on how to start an email list (where I found the quotes above) at www.smartpassiveincome.com/tutorials/how-to-start-an-email-list It's completely free, and so comprehensive you'll learn everything you need to know there.

Even master online marketer Amy Porterfield kicks herself for not building her email list sooner...

> *"'The best time to build a list was yesterday...the next best time is today.' I wish I had listened to this advice when I was just getting started with my online business."*

On an online training, Russell Brunson from ClickFunnels said that for every 1000 people you have on your list, you should be able to make at least $1000 a month in income. (And that experienced, or "good" marketers, could do even better than that.)

I've found this to be true for myself and many of my online business friends. So my question is, not when are you going to start building your list, but how fast do you want it to grow?

One way many bloggers and online business owners build their list is by giving something to a reader in exchange for that list. Often called an "opt-in" or "freebie", what you create to give away to your readers should target your ideal customer at the exact right time in their journey.

I mentioned College Geek Info earlier, and their Packing list for college freshman. While not an opt-in (and I will explain why I think it's not his actual opt-in below), it's a great example of something that could be an opt-in, because he's targeting the beginning college student, with hopes that they will stay with him and read his blog throughout his college years.

If he were to, say, have an opt-in that targeted students graduating from college, he would have missed the mark.

(By the way, most, if not all of the products he links to in that packing list are Amazon links, and you cannot use those in emails or a PDF per Amazon's rules. So that's why I believe he just offers it freely on his site... though I could be wrong.)

The point is, you want to make sure your own opt-in is targeting your ideal client and at the ideal time in their journey.

You know I love examples, so let's look at some...

If you are a food blogger that specializes in baking for beginners, you're not going to make a freebie that includes "12 brunch ideas your friends will love!" While brunch sounds great, that's not why people are visiting your site. A better opt-in might be something like, "Get my 'no-fail' dessert recipe even your pickiest friends will drool over!"

If you blog about work-at-home jobs for moms, a good freebie might be "10 Companies Hiring Remote Workers, and Tips to Help You Land the Job!"

If you blog about wedding planning, you wouldn't want your freebie to be something like "5 romantic spots to spend your first anniversary." But rather something like "5

Mistakes Newly Engaged Couples Make Planning Their Wedding (and How to Easily Avoid them!)"

Typically, these freebie opt-ins come in the form of:

- Ebooks
- Checklists
- PDFs
- Printables
- Free reports
- Worksheets
- Videos
- Audios
- Challenges
- How to's
- Discount codes
- Mini course
- Free access (to a library of goods, Facebook group, etc.)
- Kits

- Resource Guide

- Freebies list

- Workshop

- "Secrets" of your niche

- Webinar

- Etc.

Regardless of the form your opt-in eventually takes, your freebie should be something of high-value to your ideal customer (but doesn't cost a lot of you to produce and share for free), that hopefully gives them some sort of quick win so that they can quickly see you know what you're talking about and it's worth staying on your list.

Chapter 7 – Keywords & SEO Tips and Tools

SEO, or Search Engine Optimization, may sound technical and intimidating, but it doesn't have to be. The tools and tips I offer in this chapter will make it easy for you to get started and learn the essentials. Because good SEO *is* essential.

One of the reasons it's recommended that you choose a niche is because it will be helpful for both search engines and (the right) people finding you.

If you have a blog post about both camping in the winter and bathing suits, not many people are going to be interested in your topic, much less actively searching for your keywords.

So doing some keyword research *before* you write a post in your niche, and making sure that post hits all the right SEO spots as you write it and before you hit publish, you'll be setting yourself up for greater success.

First, let's go over some easy things search engines like...

Search engines like long form content. Your blog posts should have at least 900 words, and up to 1500 being even better. And, believe it or not, having a 2000-5000 word blog post could put you at the top of the search results.

Not all of your posts have to be that long! But if there are certain keywords you really want to rank for, a "long form" (what 2-5k word posts are frequently referred to as) post like that is recommended.

Search engines also like it when you use your keywords in multiple places. But adding them in to *too many* places and/or too often can have the opposite results, because then you're keyword stuffing, and that's a huge no-no.

Some good places to include your keyword phrase: the heading (or H1) of your post, the title of your post, the "slug" or the end of the URL for your post, the first paragraph, in any image alt text, any sub-headings (H2-H6), in your tags, repeated in the text of your post, in your post excerpt or snippet, etc.

That may seem like a lot to remember, and it is! Which is why I recommend using a WordPress plugin like Yoast. When you use this freemium plugin, it keeps track of all that for you.

When you're ready to hit publish, you can simply check your Yoast SEO Score (which is rated like a stoplight: Red means your SEO is really bad, Yellow means there is still some room for improvement, and Green means you're good to go!)

If your post is Red or Yellow, Yoast will give you a list of suggestions to raise your SEO Score. It will even tell you if you've used your keyword too much! (That keyword stuffing thing I mentioned earlier.)

When I first started blogging with Yoast, I really only cared about getting a yellow. But as time went on, I focused on getting more and more green lights. Now I won't hit publish until I have that green light.

So even though Yoast makes it easy (because it tells you exactly what you need to do to improve your score), don't put too much pressure on yourself in the beginning.

I use the free version of Yoast, but their paid version is affordable for most bloggers, so if you think you want to upgrade for the advanced features, go for it!

Also, Yoast is not the only WordPress plugin that helps with SEO, but it's what I use and am most familiar with. But I've heard other reputable (and big time) bloggers recommend another took called Rank Math is even better for SEO. I've decided I'll try it the next time I create a new niche site.

White Hat vs. Black Hat

In the world of SEO there are tactics that are used that are completely "legal" (in that they won't get you in trouble with search engines like Google) and ethical, and "Black Hat" that may help you grow in the search engine rankings faster and higher, but they could also get you blacklisted by Google. (And at that point, you can probably just kiss any success goodbye with that website!)

White Hat tactics are like the ideas I've shared above, as well as:

- Guest blog posting on other people's sites
- Creating something, like an infographic, that

encourages people to naturally link back to you

- Creating quality content

- Using relevant anchor text in your links

- Focus on mobile friendly content

- And more

Black Hat tactics include doing things like:

- Keyword stuffing (remember earlier when I said you don't want to add too many keywords to your posts? That is keyword stuffing.)

- Cloaking (which is basically showing one piece of content to your readers and another piece of content to search engines.)

- Paying for links to your site

- Using redirects to "trick" search engines

- Using blog comments to spam your link on multiple sites

- Private Blog Networks (which, in simple terms

means you create a bunch of blogs that link to yours in order to -falsely- look like an authority in your niche.)

The thing is, Black Hat tactics will likely get you to the top of search results. That's why even big name brands have been tempted into using them. But I never, ever suggest you try using them yourself. The risk far outweighs the reward. And we're all about creating ethical blogs that will create income for the long term, not just a season, right?!

Using Nofollow Links

Most links you include on your site are just "regular" links (a.k.a. dofollow links.) But for best SEO practices, you want to use "nofollow" links for your affiliate links.

Essentially, by adding a "nofollow" tag to your affiliate links, you're telling search engines to ignore any influence that link may have on the search results for the site you're linking to.

Sidenote: Since I talked about White Hat and Black Hat strategies, and you saw that paying for links (or using Private Blog Networks) was a definite no-no, you may have (correctly) assumed that when people link to your website, it's good for your own website's "authority". Search engines like when people add links to your site authentically (or White Hat), and they can also tell when it's being done inauthentically (or Black Hat.)

So back to our nofollow links! Search engines feel like affiliate links are biased, and don't want to use them in determining whether or not a website should be ranked higher. That's my laymen's explanation, anyway.

According to Backlinko, the definition of a nofollow link is:

"Nofollow links are links with a rel="nofollow" *HTML tag applied to them. The nofollow tag tells search engines to ignore that link. Because nofollow links do not pass PageRank they likely don't impact search engine rankings."*

Here is what a no follow link looks like in HTML:

`<a href="http://www.example.com/" rel="nofollow">Link text</a>`

Some readers may be rolling their eyes at this point, thinking, *I have to learn HTML now, too?!*

But do not fret my aspiring affiliate marketer!

Because the Internet is a magical place, and when there is a need, someone almost always comes along to fill it!

In this case, you can use a WordPress plugin to do the job for you. I've used one called Pretty Links, and it worked just fine. A little slow, but it filled my needs.

But then I found another plugin called Thirsty Affiliates, and it is amazing! Super fast, super easy to use, and (like Pretty Links) is a freemium model. But (unlike Pretty Links) the free version is so good, only a few people would even need to upgrade to the paid version. (But if you are one of those people, it has a low yearly cost.)

Doing Keyword Research

Now that you know how important keywords (and good SEO in general) are, let's talk about keyword research!

In most cases, you'll want to do keyword research before you even write your blog post. You might have a general idea about what you want to write about, but doing keyword research will help you:

- Figure out the exact title for your blog post
- Find keywords that are easier to rank for

- Find related keywords you may also want to include in your post

- Figure out how your target market actually searches for content

- And so much more!

While there are some excellent paid tools that will help you with keyword research (like SEM Rush and Ahrefs), if or when you're just starting out, you can either try their free trials and get the most out of them as you can in 7-14 days. Or you can use tools like Uber Suggest, Keywords Everywhere, Ask The Public, and/or the free Moz tools.

Of these free tools, the one I personally like best is **Keywords Everywhere** (www.keywordseverywhere.com). It's a free browser extension that works on both Chrome and Firefox browsers. It will give you keyword analysis on several search engines (like Google and Bing), but also on sites like Etsy, Amazon, YouTube, eBay and more.

It will tell you things like: how many searches your keywords get per month (or "monthly search volume"), the CPC (or Cost Per Click) advertisers are paying for one click to their websites for those keywords, and how competitive your keywords might be based on the number of advertisers running ads for those keywords.

But it also tells you things like: related keywords and a list of keywords "People Also Search for" (which is GOLDEN!)

You might start with an idea to write a blog post about "Shoes Made in the USA", and want to use that phrase as your keywords. But using Keywords Everywhere, you find that "women's shoes made in the USA" may have lower month search volume, but it's also much easier to rank for. And when you're first starting out, getting those easily ranked posts is vital!

IMPORTANT NOTE: As I was writing this, Keywords Everywhere has become a paid browser extension. But the cost is so incredibly low (probably less than $1 per month for even the most active of bloggers) I still highly recommend it.

Another free tool I use and highly recommend is the Moz Toolbar. Moz has a bunch of keyword research tools: some are free and some are not. But they're all good! Again, to begin with, using some of the free tools will help you go a long way.

One of the ways I use the Moz Tool bar is when I'm doing my keyword research, I can use it to see the domain authority (a.k.a. "DA") ranking of the sites that come up in the search results.

I'm only interested on what comes up on the first page, because so few people go beyond that page, anyway.

In order for me to feel confident I can rank on that first page for the keywords I'm considering using, I like to see at least two sites with Domain Authority (or DA) under 30. (0 is no domain authority and 100 is the highest domain authority.)

So, for my example from above, the keywords "Shoes Made in the USA" have one result with a DA of 20 (all the rest are above – or even well above 30). And the keywords "women's shoes made in the USA" have two with DA under 30, furthering my evidence that I'm more likely to get ranked for those keywords.

UberSuggest is another free keyword research tool I use from time to time. Ubersuggest can help you find hundreds of new keywords in a few minutes. They are constantly adding new features, too. It's definitely worth checking out.

I like to come up with several potential blog post topics, and then use these tools to find the perfect keywords (and niche topic) to use in future blog posts. I then keep a list of those topics so I can write about them on my blog in the future (and I never run out of ideas for what to write about!)

Chapter 8 – Affiliate Marketing with a Blog

Some people may be reading this chapter thinking, "isn't it only possible to do affiliate marketing with a blog?" And the answer is no. I go into more detail about how you can actually make money from affiliate marketing without a blog in some of the later chapters.

But for now, let's talk about affiliate marketing with a blog, because that's how *most* people will do it.

Niche Site, Authority Site, or Blog?

There may be some confusion about the difference between a niche site, an authority site, and a blog, so I want to clear that up first. But before I explain the difference, just know that the potential to make money with affiliate marketing is there for any of these types of sites.

Niche Site:

Niche sites generally have fewer pages, and a tight niche. That may seem obvious, but most websites or blogs do fall under some sort of niche.

Niche sites tend to focus on long-tail keywords that have lower searches per month, but lower competition as well. That's because they rely heavily on Google for traffic.

Niche sites can eventually grow into authority sites, if you choose to go that route.

Because they tend to be smaller, they can be easy if you're just starting out in the online business world. But also, because they're generally smaller, they tend to make less money than Authority sites or blogs.

Authority Site:

The goal of an authority site is to become the "go to" place on the internet for a specific topic. The content here should be thorough and authentic. You don't necessarily need to know everything about the subject, but you should know a lot, and be willing to outsource what you don't.

These sites will have more content than niche sites,

and not all of it will be focused on keywords or affiliate sales. Some percentage (up to half) will be more "shareable" content rather than content focused on making a sale.

However, the content that is focused on selling is usually quite long (2000-5000 words) and in-depth.

Blog:

Now, this is where it can be a little confusing, because a blog can be a niche site, or an authority site, or a more general blog. I shared a list of blog topics and niches in chapter 4, so you have a good idea of what some of the more general topics could be.

Let's use parenting as a topic. You could have a general parenting blog. Or you could make it into an authority blog if you made it into something like, a blog about single parenting. Or parenting teenagers. You could niche down even further and make it a niche site about potty training toddlers.

Plus, blogs will typically rely on a variety of traffic sources: from Google and other search engines, to social media, paid advertising, Pinterest, YouTube, their email list, and more.

Niche Site, Authority Site, or Blog Income Differences?

Here's the thing: no one, myself included, can guarantee that you'll make money online. Like, any at all. But the potential is certainly there!

What I will say is this: I think you should be prepared to work on your website (no matter which type you choose) for 6 to 12 months before seeing any income, much less profit.

That may seem like a long time, but let's put it in perspective, shall we?

You can start a blog for under $1000... (probably under $100 if you can do it yourself.) But most people will start off spending around $500 in the first one to six months. You can work on your site any time of the day or night, anywhere you have internet access (and sometimes you won't even need that! Like when you're writing articles or creating graphics.) And, if you do it right, you should start to see some sales in the first 3 months or so... it's just that they might be a little as $2.64 in one month like one of my niche sites did!

But let's get real...

Compare that, to say, starting a local gift shop in your town, filled with products made by locals. You still get to handpick what you sell, but you need to come up with rent for your space (first and last, if not more), plus all the displays, the actual inventory, employees, insurance, signage, electricity, advertising, marketing, etc. etc. Your monthly expenses alone would probably be *at least* $2000, which means you'd have to sell at least $4000 in products every month, just to break even! And that's just on your monthly expenses, not to mention your start-up expenses. That's also not even including paying yourself or considering how many hours a week you'll have to be physically in that space, away from family, friends, and home.

Vs. spending <$100-$1000 in start-up costs on a blog, and working the hours you can (when the kids are sleeping or after your 9 to 5, etc.) Sounds pretty awesome, am I right?

So let's look at some of your next steps, along with start-up costs…

But first: It should go without saying, once you have these things, you won't need to go out and buy/pay for them again. (Unless you want to start a new site from scratch, then by all means…) Also, I will have links to all of these resources (and more) in the book bonus PDF.

Domain Name

I buy my domain names from NameCheap.com. Not only are the domains themselves inexpensive (just like the name implies!), but they also offer free WHOIS Guard, which means your information is private (otherwise, anyone can look up and see a domain name owner's name, address, phone number, email address, as more.)

Typical cost: Under $10 per year.

Hosting

For hosting (which is where your domain and blog "live") I use and recommend SiteGround. Their starter plans are affordable, and their customer support, up-time, and site speed are all above average in my experience. I've tried other hosting companies (including NameCheap.com, because they offer hosting, too), but so far SiteGround is where I've been happiest.

Typical starter cost: $4-$6 per month when pre-paid annually.

WordPress

Once you have your hosting account set up with SiteGround, you'll want to install WordPress, which is totally free.

Website Themes

Once WordPress is installed, you'll need to choose a theme. You can get free themes right there in your WordPress dashboard through SiteGround, or you might want to "upgrade" to something nicer and/or faster (site load time is vitally important!)

I like Generate Press because you can get it for free (although I recommend upgrading to the Premium version), and it's super fast to load and easy to use.

Website Design

To make designing your site even easier, I use and recommend a WordPress plugin called ElementorPro. It makes creating fast, beautiful websites SO easy. It's drag and drop designing, so even your 12 year old can create a beautiful, optimized site. (Oh, who am I kidding?! They could probably make one already!)

WordPress Plugins

There are literally tens of thousands of WordPress plugins. These plugins are meant to make your website better, in some way or another. But don't be fooled, some will actually hurt your website and/or slow it down. So even though it can feel like you're a kid in a candy store, I urge you to use restraint when it comes to installing new plugins.

I do, however, recommend the following plugins for all WordPress blogs:

- Thirsty Affiliates (for affiliate marketing)

- Yoast (for SEO)

- Tasty Pins (for promoting on Pinterest)

- Milotree (for getting social media followers)

- A plugin that allows you to add header and footer tags

- Google Analytics Dashboard for WP (to easily keep an eye on your analytics)

- A pop-up to get people on your email list (this may or may not involve a plugin)

Writing Content for Your Blog

Once you have the "bones" or your blog set up, you'll need to start filling it in with content.

If you're a brand new blogger, I've heard that you should have as few as five blog posts to start, but up to as many as fifty if you really want to start with a bang! That seems a bit intimidating to me, and just to give you an idea, I started my most recent blog with 8 posts. I do think more is typically better, but if it's holding you back from getting started, just push publish and launch.

Yes, you might make mistakes from time to time, but that's the only way to learn how to do this thing called online business!

If your writing skills aren't as sharp as you'd like

them to be, I will say that they will likely get better with time. While I'm nowhere near perfect, I have come so far from my first several blog posts way back when. In fact, even in the last year my writing has continued to improve, as will yours.

But there are ways to get around this, if you really feel like you aren't a great writer.

One is to just write like you're writing to a friend or loved one. I do this all the time, including the writing of this book! It takes away any stuffiness and creates a warm and friendly tone.

Of course, your blog may require something other than a friendly tone. Maybe you want to be more business-like. Or funny. Etc. In that case, think of your ideal customer (or customer avatar as it's also called) as you write.

Another is to hire out the writing for your blog. This can get pretty expensive, but if you don't have the talent and/or the time to write every post yourself, hiring a freelance writer is a great option. I do this all the time. Mostly because I don't have a lot of time, and I have tons of content ideas.

There are several places to find writers. Some

suggestions are:

- Content Development Pros
- Upwork
- The ProBlogger Job Board
- The Urban Writers
- E-Writer Solutions

There are tons of sites out there, from cheap to very expensive. I typically pay a fair, mid-range price for my extra blog posts. I've tried out cheap services like Fiverr, and it really is true what they say: you get what you pay for. I basically had to re-write the entire article.

You can also have people guest post on your blog. You can offer to pay for posts, or you can simply post their article without payment but in exchange they get free exposure and a link back to their site. (Which is great for SEO!)

But the truth is, in most cases you'll likely be doing most of the writing yourself. If you'd rather talk, you could start a podcast. And if you prefer video, you could start a YouTube channel. And you could make affiliate income via those avenues! But we're talking about blogging here, so let's talk about content...

Content is just what it sounds like: the stuff we put in blog posts. Affiliate blog posts can be about one product, or many, but it should have a main theme.

For instance, a food blogger would write a blog post about one recipe, not several in the same post. They could include affiliate links for the food, tools, etc.

Even a lifestyle blogger may write about a broad subject (say, the day in the life of a digital nomad in Lisbon) so they could include affiliate links for a variety of products as well, but there is still a general theme to their post.

But say you have a review site. You wouldn't review five different mascaras and three different types of vacuums in the same post. It just doesn't make sense – to your readers or to search engines.

I'll cover specific topics and types of posts in the next chapter. Until then, let's talk more about content.

Content Schedule

Once your site is up and running, it's good to have a content schedule. Depending on what type of blog you have, you may want to schedule posts according to seasons or events. For example, if you're a wedding blogger, you'll want to schedule wedding ideas for each season. If you're a food blogger, you will want to schedule (at least some) posts around holidays or events (like football games, etc.)

Or you may want to schedule posts based on certain affiliate programs themselves. For instance, Marie Forleo only offers her signature B-School program once a year (typically in February.) If you are one of her affiliates, you'll know you want to start creating content that will support that launch in January and February.

You may also want to schedule content around your own schedule. By that I mean, if you sell your own product (with or even without the help of your own affiliates) you know you'll need to write content to support that launch, too.

In addition to having a content schedule, I always have a running list of content ideas that I add to any time an idea strikes. Or if I've simply done some keyword research and found a few new golden nuggets.

I simply use a paper planner and Dynalist (a

freemiuim, modern and lightweight outliner that you can use on a desktop computer and/or as an app on your phone) to keep track of when and what to publish on your blog.

When You Don't Need to Write a Full Blog Post

There will be times when you don't actually need to write a full blog post. In those cases, you can simply create a landing page, or a squeeze page.

There are several tools that will help you do this. You could just use ElementorPro (the web design plugin I mentioned earlier). Or you could use software like Kartra, LeadPages, or Clickfunnels. I've used all three, and decided Elementor works best for me. I believe they all offer free trials, so you can try them out yourself, too.

The point of a landing page like this is to simply convince the person who goes there to give you their email address in exchange for something else. This could be a freebie you've created (like a checklist, ebook, upgrade, discount code, audio, etc.), or a video training, webinar, etc. that will teach them something they really want to know, etc.

The thing is, you can also create a landing page for affiliate offers. Rather than send them directly to the affiliate's site, it's best to get their email address first, so you can also follow up with them.

I do this with affiliate products that have evergreen webinars, launches, or freebie offers they've come up with as well.

But the most important part is that I get them on my email list first. Because in affiliate marketing, the fortune is in the follow up, and email is by far the easiest and more effective way to not only follow up, but to build trust with your readers.

Advertising

I'm not going to do a deep dive into advertising, because that could honestly be a book in itself (one I may end up writing at a later date.) But I want to touch on it here because many successful affiliate marketers drive traffic directly to affiliate sales pages with great success.

I know many use ads on sites like Facebook, Bing, Instagram, etc. Wherever you may try advertising, it's important to know your ROI – or return on investment.

That's basically a way for marketers to gauge how much money they made minus the money they spent to make that money.

For example, let's say I'm an affiliate for XYZ company, and I make $100 commission for every person I send to them who buys.

That means I can spend up to $99 driving traffic to them and I'd still make a dollar (this, in my opinion, is not a great ROI, but I'll explain how it might work in some instances in a bit).

So then I have to figure out how many leads I have to send to them in order to make a sale. Let's say (for the ease of math!), on average if I send them 100 leads, I get one sale. That's $1 per lead I send them, and I'm just barely making my investment back.

Now, everyone has to figure out their own comfort zone for advertising. I personally would feel much more comfortable spending $50 (or less of, course!) to earn that $100 commission.

But there is a way to ensure you make even more than that one time, $100 commission, and this is my "secret sauce" to affiliate marketing.

Well, it's neither a secret or a sauce, but it definitely helps me make more affiliate income!

And that is simply setting up a landing page (or squeeze page) that I set up where I tease the affiliate offer – but they have to enter their name and email address in order to go on to the next page. I might even offer my own freebie if they sign up.

Now, please check GDPR and other current laws before implementing this type of landing page, because it has to be set up in a very specific way in order to be compliant. You'll also want to make sure your FTC affiliate disclosures (that we went over in a previous chapter) are also in place on this landing page.

But by getting this prospect (that you're paying for, anyway!) onto your email list *before* you send them onto the affiliate offer, you're able to stay in touch with them, and sell to them again and again.

So even if they do or don't buy the offer you're sending them to, there is still a potential ROI for that person.

I want to take a step back here and just add this: All

this talk of ROI and leads and advertising and selling... well, it all makes it sound a bit cold to me. I just want to reiterate that **I believe that affiliate marketing is a beautiful, mutually beneficial way to share things with others/your audience that can truly have a positive impact on their lives when done right.**

I understand that some people will sell just to make a commission.

But that's not my style or what I'm trying to teach you here. I believe that, when done with integrity and values, affiliate marketing can be even more powerful than just a one-time commission. You can actually build trust and relationships with the people you're serving.

I truly hope that's how you incorporate affiliate marketing into your own blog or business, as well.

Chapter 9 - Highly Effective, Yet Underused Affiliate Ideas

So how do you actually use your affiliate links on your blog? There are plenty of ways. Most people start by just randomly adding them into blog posts. It's not the worst way to start, but it's also not the most effective.

Let's talk about more effective ways to include affiliate links in your blog!

If you already have a blog, do this first

If you already have a blog, check your Google Analytics and find your top five to ten current blog posts. Once you've identified those, go through them one by one (starting with the most popular and working your way down this list) and see how you might incorporate affiliate links into those posts.

You know you're already getting traffic to those posts, so *why not* monetize them with affiliate links. Plus, this will give you an idea for what types of affiliate programs and networks you'll want to sign up with.

Tutorials

Tutorials on how to use a specific product or software are a terrific way to get people to buy through your affiliate link – as long as you set them up properly.

Think about it, in most cases, someone looking for a tutorial on a specific product probably already owns that product.

So your tutorial needs to be positioned in a way that targets people *before* they purchase. I'll give you some examples so you can see what I mean, and create your tutorial accordingly.

Let's say you're creating a tutorial for the email service provider, ConvertKit. You may want to title that post something like, *Why ConvertKit is Better Than Mailchimp (including a mini tutorial)*.

If you are a food blogger and you want to demonstrate how to use an Instant Pot®, your tutorial post could be called *Instant Pot® vs. a Pressure Cooker: Learn How*

Easy an Instant Pot® Can Be.

As you can see, these examples will draw in people who have not yet made the purchase, which is exactly where you want them to be, so they ultimately buy through your affiliate link.

YouTube & Video

If you can create your tutorials, etc., on video, even better. Not only can you put them on YouTube, which has a huge audience, for increased exposure, but you can also imbed them into your own blog posts. YouTube makes it super easy: all you have to do is add a line of code to your post.

Videos could include you showing how to use whatever it is you're creating an affiliate for, or simply a video of your screen as you use/teach/or demonstrate the product. Or, personally I think it's ideal to include both.

But I'm a bit camera shy myself, so for the most part, my videos are screen only. I guess this is a case of *"do as I say, not as I do."* But honestly, I think you just have to figure out what is right for you and your business.

If you're going to put your videos on YouTube,

remember that it's actually a search engine. So treat your video sort of like you would a blog post: come up with a keyword rich title and description, without going overboard and being keyword spammy.

Also remember to disclose your affiliate links on YouTube. I like to mention it in the video itself, as well as in the video description. You'll want to do the same on your site, as with every other post or page on your site that includes affiliate links.

Before & After Posts

Before and after posts are a great way to include affiliate links, and not just for home makeovers! (Although, those are fun, too!)

This could include before and after ideas like:

- Office/kitchen/bathroom/etc. organization

- Using an anti-aging product after 30 days

- Cleaning out and organizing a closet

- Your fridge before and after you start a veggie juice cleanse

- Your website before and after installing a new

WordPress theme

- Your email newsletter design before and after switching to a new service provider

- Before and after you wash your dog with an organic dog shampoo

- Before and after a weight loss or fitness journey

- Makeup vs no makeup

- Before and after using whitening strips on your teeth

- Before and after cleaning your bathtub with a certain product

- Etc.

Obviously, not all of these ideas will fit all blogs. But hopefully they will, at the very least, inspire some before and after ideas for *your* blog.

Interview the Maker/Owner/Creator

This is one of my favorite ways to include affiliate links in a post. Because it not only introduces your readers to the product, but also the person or people behind the product.

You know I love giving you examples of how you might use these ideas, so let's jump right to them!

If you have a favorite artist on Etsy, you could interview them and include affiliate links in the images of their work.

You could interview the creator of a course you took and loved.

Sometimes even the owners/creators or the software you use are available to interview.

If you love a certain book, you could interview the author (especially if they're an indie or new author).

There's a handmade tool that I use for a craft I enjoy (and blog about) and I interviewed the makers of the tool. It was so nice to get to know the people behind the tool, knowing how much time and attention to detail, and, quite frankly, love they put into creating it.

I think that's why these interviews are awesome: they provide a connection between your reader and the maker, which can help them decide to purchase.

But as an alternative, you could interview people

who also use the product or service. Or at least include short (or long!) quotes from them about why they love it so much, how it's made their lives easier/better, etc.

Have a Resources or "Tools" Page

I feel like my resources page is the unsung hero of my site. It's in the top ten (or even five) of my most visited pages on my site, which means it earns a lot of affiliate income.

So, for just about any blogging niche, you could have a tools and/or resources page of your own.

If you blog about business, you could include your favorite and most used tools.

If you blog about makeup, you could have a list of essential makeup items no one should be without.

If you blog about parties, you could share a list of things no party should start without.

If you blog about bullet journaling, you could have a list of basic bujo tools for people who are just getting started.

Whatever it is you blog about, there are certainly some fundamental items your readers should have in order to do what you're doing, or learn what you're teaching. Including them in this kind of list on a prominent page on your site is a true service to your readers.

In Your Podcast

If you have a podcast, you can include both "shout out" affiliate links in the show and/or affiliate links in the show notes.

This is especially great if you're a new(er) podcaster and you don't have the download numbers for paid advertisers, yet. You can be your own "advertiser" and simply use affiliate links so that when people go buy through them, you earn a commission.

I'd definitely recommend using a plugin like Thirsty Affiliates to shorten the affiliate URLs to something like: www.YourDomain.com/AffilateCo and I'd even mention the URL itself several times. That way it's easier for the person listening to remember.

You can simply mention that it's an affiliate link and it helps support the show. People want to support you that way when you're offering them such good advice, entertainment, etc.

And of course you'll want to include the link in your show notes, where it will also live on the podcast player(s) that you publish on, as well as your website.

Even if you have sponsors for your show, sometimes being your own sponsor can be even more lucrative for you. Especially when you promote recurring affiliate programs.

But beyond the sponsorship idea, you could also combine some of the other ideas I've mentioned: like interviewing the maker of a software product. Or the teacher of a course. Or an artist or craftsperson who sells on a platform that has an affiliate program.

You could also interview people who took a certain course about their experience with it. Or someone who switched from one software company to another (and why they did it, how easy or difficult it was, how happy they are with their decision, etc.)

But I also have another idea that you could incorporate in your podcast (or not, if you don't have one!) And that is…

Offering your Own Bonuses

If you have a product, course, ebook, etc. that compliments what you're also trying to sell as an affiliate, you might want to offer it/them as incentive for people to not only buy what you're promoting, but buy it through your specific link.

I've seen this used on higher-ticket items. If you've ever heard of B-School you've probably seen this in action. B-School is pretty pricey (it was $1999 when I took it.) Affiliates earn a 50% commission, so they are willing to either create bonuses specifically for the people who buy through their link, or they offer their own programs (which may cost as much as B-School itself!) as a free bonus.

In fact, the B-School affiliates are so generous with their free bonuses, some savvy people "shop around" to find the bonus they really want and then buy through that affiliate.

But even if you're promoting a product that is, say $97, you might want to create a free ebook or mini-course to giveaway as a free bonus to the people who buy through you.

Here are some words of warning, however: you

might want to wait to give them their bonus until after the refund period on the product you're an affiliate for. That way they don't just get your product for free, because you (might not) have a way to refuse them access to it once you've given it to them.

You can explain it as simply as that: *You will receive my bonus after making sure you're happy with your original purchase for 14 (or 30 or 60, etc.) days.*

Or, if the thing they're buying is, say, a six week course, you can tell them that you don't want to overwhelm them, and that you will be sending them their bonuses once the course is over. Obviously, you want to be clear and explain that before they buy through you. Because you certainly don't want to upset your customers by telling them that after the fact.

Other Ways to Include Affiliate Links

There are some more common ways to include affiliate links and I want to share them with you here, too, so you never run out of ideas for affiliate posts.

Round-Ups

Round-up posts are one of the most popular ways to

include affiliate links. Think:

- 20 Sweaters You Must Have for Fall
- 21 Gifts for Your Friend Who is Turning 21
- 30 Engagement Rings She'll Love to Say YES to
- The Best Sketchbooks for Budding Cartoonists
- 7 Kitchen Gadgets You Didn't Know You Needed
- 8 All-Natural Sugar Substitutes
- Etc.

Checklists

Checklists are another popular way to include affiliate links. Think:

- What to Pack for Your First Backpacking Trip
- Must-Have Bachelorette Party Supplies
- What Every New Fisherman Needs Before Their First Trip
- Minimalist Wardrobe Staples
- Every New Parent Should Have These in Their

Diaper Bag

- Classroom Essentials for Brand New Teachers
- Etc.

Share Your Experience

This idea is pretty obvious, because I encourage you to promote affiliate products that you already use and love. But again, not every blogger can actually do that.

Like a bridal blogger. You could (hopefully) only write about one dress, but you may want to blog about many dresses for many wedding seasons. In that case, obviously you're not going to have personal experience with each dress.

But you might have an experience you could share about the one dress you did choose. You could talk about how and why you chose it, how it felt to wear on your wedding day, etc. And while you could include the exact dress in your post, you could also include some "look alike" dresses, or dresses in a similar style.

But if you've taken a course, read a book, used a certain type of paint in your paintings... these are all examples of things you could write about your experience with.

List Posts

These can be similar to both the round-up posts and the checklist posts, but they can also be different! Like:

- Top Ten 1980s Horror Films
- The 6 Best Hiking Boots for Women
- 12 Cute Office Supplies
- 8 Facial Masks Your Skin Will Love
- 10 Books for 10 Year Old Girls
- 6 Ways to Clean Your Bathroom Quickly
- Etc.

Series Posts

I like series posts because they can be more than one post for your website (which means repeat visitors if people love what you're teaching.) Some ideas include:

- Budgeting for … (new parents, college students, new business owners, etc.)

- How I Started (and Kept on) Juicing (week one, week two, month one, etc.)

- Meditation for ... (writers, artists, single dads, etc.)

- How to Start a Lifestyle Blog Series

- Etc.

This vs. That

I talked a bit about this before, but if you have experience with two different (but competing) products, a "this vs. that" type post is a great way to help people – who are looking to buy something right then – decide which way to go.

In these posts, be honest: which means you'll want to praise, and criticize, both products. Share as much detail as you can, so your readers can get a full picture of what they (might be!) buying.

How To:

How to posts are similar to demo posts, but in this case, you'll be covering more than just how to use one particular thing. So you could teach people:

- How to Build a Backyard Water Fountain

- How to Create a Course that Sells

- How to Paint Your Face Like a Fawn for Halloween

- How to Figure Out What Makeup Colors Look Best on You

- How to Travel Cheaply

- How to Use a Weaving Loom

- How to Bake a Flourless Cake

- Etc.

The Ultimate Guide To...

If you're going to create an "ultimate guide" to something, be prepared to work on it for a while. These posts could be 5000 to 10,000 words (that's about 1/3 of this entire book!), or more. And they may or may not include helpful photos and/or videos to help your readers fully understand the subject.

Some Ultimate Guide topics include:

- The Ultimate Guide to Wedding Planning

- The Ultimate Guide to Keto Dieting

- The Ultimate Guide to Puppy Training

- The Ultimate Guide to Baking the Perfect Pie

- The Ultimate Guide to Writing Your First Novel

- The Ultimate Guide to Austin, TX

- Etc.

Reviews

You can review products, courses, books, (or even services) you've tried. You could review one particular thing in your post, or several of the same variety. For instance:

- My Honest Review of XYZ Course

- I Paid Someone to Write Blog Posts for Me and This Happened

- 10 Books I Read This Year That Changed Me

- 5 Lipsticks Over $50 That are Worth Every Penny

- I Tried XYZ for 30 Days and THIS is What Happened

- I Taste-tested 9 Protein Shakes and My Favorite

Was...

- Etc.

Hopefully by now you have so many ideas for affiliate blog posts, you'll never run out! But blogging isn't the only way to make money with affiliate marketing. So in the next few chapters I'll share even more ideas.

Chapter 10 - Affiliate Marketing in Email

Having an opt-in email list is one of the surest ways you can make money with affiliate marketing. Statistics show that email outperforms just about everything: paid ads, social media, blog content, and even offline marketing and more. (See Email ROI in the references section.)

But how do you get those people on your email list? And even more importantly, how do you keep them there?

First, let's talk about "opting in."

All About Opt-ins

I want to make sure you understand what an email "opt-in" is.

Basically, someone has to agree to receive emails from you, and you must offer a way for them to stop receiving emails from you within every email you send.

Usually, that looks something like this:

A person comes to your blog (or landing page – which I'll get into detail about later) and at some point they see a form to subscribe to your email list.

If/when they enter their name (typically, though it's not required unless you want it to be) and email address, that is considered a "single opt-in."

If you and/or your email service provider requires them to then click on a link in the first email they get from you to "confirm" that they really, truly want to be a subscriber, that is considered a "double opt-in."

There are advantages and disadvantages to both.

The advantages of the single opt-in are that you get more people on your list. This is great, especially if you want to grow your list quickly.

The disadvantages of the single opt-in are that some people will not remember subscribing and consider your emails spam. Single opt-ins also may not be "legal" in some parts of the world.

The advantages of a double opt-in email list are that you're more likely to have a more engaged, compliant list.

Plus email service providers generally charge you based on how many subscribers you have, and you really only want to pay for those who truly want to receive your emails.

The disadvantages of a double opt-in email list are that, well, your list might grow more slowly because people will sometimes forget to confirm, change their minds, and/or the confirmation email may end up in their Spam folder without them ever realizing it.

Overall, it's considered "best practice" to have a double opt-in list. I've tried both and having a double opt-in list is my preference, as well.

Email Marketing Services

There are many email marketing services out there for bloggers and/or online entrepreneurs - at every level.

Email marketing services (or EMSs for short), have many advantages, like:

- They can help you deliver free goods to incentivize people to subscribe (aka Lead Magnets, which I'll go over in more detail later in this chapter)

- They can handle large numbers of emails being sent

- They can help you customize your emails with things like a person's name

- They can help you "tag" subscribers for different things, like where are they in their journey you're helping them with (beginner to advanced), whether or not they have purchased anything from you, etc.

- They can track things like: email open rates, clicks on individual lists, sales, etc.

- They can help you automate your customer follow up

- And more!

There are tons of EMSs to choose from. I personally like ConvertKit as a standalone EMS, and Kartra (that includes an EMS with a bunch of other products, like landing page builders, check out forms, membership forms, helpdesks, calendars, affiliate programs for your products, etc.) If you love to send image-heavy, gorgeous emails, I recommend FloDesk.

But popular Email Marketing Services include:
- ConvertKit

- Kartra

- Aweber

- FloDesk

- ConstantContact

- Keap (formerly InfusionSoft)

- Emma

- Drip

- ActiveCampaign

- GetResponse

- MailChimp (though they do not allow affiliate marketing in their emails. Same with another company called MailerLite.)

In the end, you'll have to choose one that is right for you and your unique business.

Building Your Email List

Once you've chosen an email marketing service, you'll want to start building your email list.

Some people may think that an email list won't be necessary for their niche, but in almost all cases, I would disagree. "*The money is in the list*" as they say!

But to be fair, there are some niches that may not need an email list.

How do you know if your niche is one of them?

By testing. I know it's not necessarily fun, but you'll want to start and grow your email list regardless of your niche.

Some people say that you should be earning about (or at least) $1 per month for every person on your email list. So if you have 1000 subscribers, you should be making $1000 per month from that list alone.

Having a list (or rather, having an EMS) costs money. So if you have a list of 1000 people, and you're paying $29 a month to email them, it should be fairly easy to not only recoup your expenses, but to make a profit, as well.

But if you have a list of 50,000 people and you're paying $400 a month for your EMS, you'll really want to make sure you're covering your expenses, plus making money on it.

I had a list once with 6000 (give or take) people on it,

and it was earning me exactly $0 every month... except for one month when I did an affiliate launch and I made $1000. I was paying $99 a month to email that list for over two years. Obviously, my return on investment was negative, even if you spread out that income over the two years.

I scrubbed that list, getting rid of all the "bad" emails (emails that bounced, subscribers that hadn't opened my emails in months, etc.) After that it was down to under 2000, and I could justify paying for it at that point. But mostly because I really wanted to keep the email list. (And I'm glad I did! After I scrubbed it I finally started making money with it.)

So that's what you'll have to do, too: build the email list (to at least 1000 subscribers, I'd say) and see if it's worth the cost.

So how do you build your email list?

There are several ways. Typically, your EMS will provide you with a way to include a subscription form and/or a landing page for your website. Most EMS's offer integration with WordPress at the very least. Others will work on different platforms, like Squarespace, Weebly, Wix, etc.

You should definitely have a page on your site dedicated entirely to getting people to opt-in to your email list. Then link that page with a "subscribe" button in a variety of places: your top menu, your footer menu, on your "about" and "contact" pages, in your sidebar, etc.

You can also add pop-up forms on your site. Some people love them, some people hate them, but after tons of testing and more testing the facts are in: they work.

Some people like to have a large "welcome mat" email subscription form, and I know they can work. But I also know that, when I go to someone's site for the first time, that big subscription form is shouting at me: *"You don't know me yet, but give me your email address, anyway!"*

Unless they're offering something SO good I just can't say no, I usually pass on subscribing at that point.

Which is one of the reasons I prefer an "exit intent" pop-up. They work like this: if someone is on your site, and by the way they are moving their mouse (usually towards the "back" button or to close the tab entirely) a form will pop up and ask them to subscribe.

At that point, they've at least gotten to know what your site is about a little bit, and maybe a bit about you, too.

But they're leaving anyway (or at least the pop-up software thinks they are), so why *not* ask for their email, in one last ditch effort to get them on your list?

The thing is, you could, and should, test to see which one works best on your site. You may prefer one over the other, but the real choice should be made by your website visitors.

Without a Website

You can actually build an email list without a website. So if you don't have one or don't even want one, you can still build a list.

There are a couple of ways to do this.

You can simply use the email landing page(s) that your EMS offers. The downside to this is you (typically) get really weird/funky URLs when you just use their landing pages. Something like:

https://1234nid.ems.com/jjoptin.html

That doesn't make sense, nor is it easy to share.

That's why I recommend still buying a domain, at the very least, and plugging in your landing page there. That way the URL above can instead be something like:

https://YourAwesomeDomain.com

I know I said "without a website" and this kind of sounds like you have a website. In some ways, that's true. You'll need the domain name, a host and some sort of way to install that EMS landing page onto the site (like Wordpress.org).

But that doesn't require you to build out an entire site, with an about page, a blog, etc. It's essentially a one-page site, that simply consists of your landing page.*

*You may be required to have a few other pages on that site for legal reasons, which we will go over in more detail in Chapter 13.

Lead Magnet Ideas

A lead magnet (also, confusingly, called an "opt-in" or opt-in bribe) is basically a gift of some sort that you give to someone for subscribing to your emails.

There are tons of things you could give away in order to incentivize someone to subscribe. Here is a list of starter ideas:

- Ebook

- Printables
- Video training
- Audio
- A chapter of your book
- Calendar
- Workbook
- Spreadsheet
- A summary of a blog post
- Checklist
- Quiz results
- An audiobook (or a chapter of one)
- Art (for their phone, desktop, or even printable)
- Insider secrets
- A discount or coupon code
- Access to a member's only area
- Cheat sheet
- Template

- A free webinar
- Toolkit
- Insider Resources
- Free shipping offer
- Etc.

No matter which type of lead magnet you choose to create, there are a few things to consider. Ask yourself:

Will this give my reader a "quick win"? You want your lead magnet to be quick and easy to implement, providing your reader a win that they will remember.

Will this be incentive enough for them to subscribe? Your lead magnet shouldn't be something they can very easily make themselves or find elsewhere on the internet for free. Make it of value.

Does it show off your expertise? If you're a coach for women bloggers over 50, you'll want to make sure that your lead magnet helps women bloggers over 50 specifically and with confidence and proficiency.

Is it on brand? If your lead magnet is about Facebook Ads but your site is about traveling on a budget, you need to think again.

Will it help your reader at the beginning of your funnel? Say you have a wedding blog. You want to offer a lead magnet that gets your ideal customer, at the ideal time... like right after they've said "yes" to a proposal. That way you grab them just as they start to plan their big day.

That is really important, so I want to offer another example: Say you blog about blogging, and your biggest affiliate offer is a website hosting plan. Well, you want to find *potential* bloggers – those that don't even have a web host yet.

So rather than a "How to use XYZ Hosting" opt-in, something like "7 Secrets You Must Know Before Getting a Host for Your New Blog."

You want to catch them right *before* they take the next step, which will include buying something via your affiliate link, rather than after they have already purchased it.

Important to Note

Once they're on your list you're going to be sending them emails (obviously!) But here's the thing: some affiliate programs do not allow you to use affiliate links in your emails.

Amazon is a BIG one.

I mean, just about anyone who does affiliate marketing online is going to join Amazon's affiliate program at some point! And Amazon says it's a BIG no-no to include their affiliate links in your emails.

You may see other people doing it anyway. Maybe they don't realize it's against the rules. Maybe they do, and just want to take the chance. Either way, it doesn't really matter. The point is, you don't want to break this rule.

It can be difficult to know when email links are okay or not (those terms & conditions pages can be as long as War and Peace and as dry as the desert!) If you have any questions whether or not you can use them, try contacting your affiliate manager (if they have one) for an answer.

If you know it's not okay to use affiliate links in your emails, or you're just not sure if they're okay or not (and you don't want to risk it), include links to your website where a). the affiliate link(s) are and b). you've included the proper disclosures.

What are "proper disclosures"?

I covered proper disclosures in Chapter 3, so in case you skipped that one because it seemed dry and boring... well, first of all: I don't blame you! But second of all, it's really, *really* important (like, your-business-hangs-in-the-balance-important). So just give it a quick read and make sure to include the proper disclosures.

But because we're talking specifically about email, I thought it was important to note that you must disclose your affiliate links here, too. Not just on your blog, but in your emails, social media posts, pins on Pinterest, your YouTube videos, webinars, live videos... any and everywhere, really. If it's an affiliate link, make sure you say so.

What do you do once people are on your list?

I used to send people a welcome email that introduced me and my business and that was it. From there they'd simply get my weekly emails.

But I've since learned it's a good idea to have a welcome sequence – not just one email, but many, sent over several days or even weeks (or months, if you feel up to it!)

Your welcome sequence (all set up and automated in your EMS) might look something like this:

Email 1: sent immediately after your new lead confirms their subscription.

In this email you'll generally deliver your lead magnet and welcome them to your list. You might want to add a few notes, like how happy you are to have them, and some of the types of emails they can expect to receive from you.

Email 2: sent one day after they've confirmed their subscription.

This email can be a follow up about the lead magnet you've given them, and/or an introduction to you and your business.

Email 3: sent two days after the last email.

In this email you might ask them to tell you a little more about them. Where are they at this point in their journey. How can you best help them, etc.

Email 4: sent three days after the last email.

This might be the first email you send that actually tries to sell them something. Before that you're simply warming them up, both letting them get to know you, and vice versa. Now that they're more comfortable with you,

you could tell them about a great deal, your favorite affiliate offer, or how you use XYZ and they might want it, too, etc.

Your welcome series could go on and on like this... from offering free, valuable information to selling them something, on repeat as long as you'd like. But you don't want to overwhelm them with offers, so just make sure you're adding value first and most often, then pitching to them.

The one exception to this that I can think of is if you have an affiliate site that links to mostly ecommerce sites (like fashion blogs, beauty blogs, travel blogs, pet blogs, etc.). In that case, people are going there to buy, so you can definitely do more selling. Recipe or cooking blogs could send out more emails with sales pitches, too.

Because you'll also be sending your regular weekly emails along with these automated welcome emails, you just want to make sure you're not overwhelming anyone.

A balance of sales and nurturing emails is almost always going to be the most effective and appreciated way of connecting with your readers.

One more note before we move on... Some people

will be nervous about sending this many emails. They will worry that it's too much, that they don't want to be pushy or salesy.

First of all, if you're worried that you'll be too pushy or salesy, you probably won't be. But if you do worry, well, just don't be pushy. Back off. Rein it in. You'll probably know if you've gone too far.

But also, because you're blogging and doing affiliate marketing in an honest, respectable way, people will be drawn to you.

Or I should say: the RIGHT people will be drawn to you. If Pat Flynn sent me three emails a day I still wouldn't unsubscribe. Because I look forward to what he has to say, and I know I'll learn from him (even in a "sales email.")

If someone unsubscribed from your list, don't worry about it! They weren't the right people for you in the first place.

Just keep your mind and your messages on the people who ARE your biggest fans. Keep nurturing them and they will stand by your side.

Chapter 11 - Affiliate Marketing on Pinterest

I think affiliate marketing on Pinterest is brilliant! Partly because it's easy to do, and also because you don't even need a website to do it. Having said that, I feel like I need to disclose a few things before we get into the "how to's" of doing affiliate marketing on Pinterest.

First and foremost, check the current rules about affiliate marketing on Pinterest. They used to allow it, then they banned it for a few years, and, as of the moment I'm writing this book, it's okay to do.

As far as Pinterest rules go, some general guidelines (again, as of the time I'm writing this) are:

Don't use link shorteners like bit.ly – Pinterest doesn't allow them. Some affiliate programs will give you the option to shorten links. It's unclear if Pinterest allows those, but to be on the safe side, always use the long (and, I know) ugly links they provide.

The same goes for cloaked links or redirects. Pinterest usually marks those as spam, even if they're not going to an affiliate link.

You must disclose all affiliate links in the Pin description. Even if you have an affiliate disclosure on the page you're linking to (and you should!) you still need to disclose it in the Pin description itself. You can use a hashtag, like #affiliatelink or even simply #ad. Or just include the words "affiliate link" in the description.

Those are some general guidelines when it comes to using affiliate links on Pinterest. To learn more directly from Pinterest, please visit:

https://policy.pinterest.com/en/community-guidelines

But don't just check with Pinterest! Check with the companies you're an affiliate for, too. Some are happy to have you pin affiliate links directly (like I'm going to teach you later in this chapter.) But others (like Amazon and Etsy, to mention a couple) strictly do not allow it.

It also depends on what country you're in. Like I

mentioned, Amazon doesn't allow direct affiliate links on Pinterest... in the U.S. BUT it appears that you can have them if you're in the EU (see https://amazon-affiliate.eu/en/affiliate-links-allowed-pinterest/).

Yes, it can be confusing. But it's important that you understand and follow the rules. Just saying "I didn't know I wasn't allowed to do that!" probably won't get your suspended affiliate account back up and running.

You also can't use the excuse that you saw other pinners doing it. Trust me, you will see other pinners breaking the rules. But that doesn't mean it's okay, or that they won't get caught, eventually.

Now that you know the general rules, the next thing to do is to sign up for a business account on Pinterest, if you haven't already. It's free to do and will only take a few minutes.

Start by going to https://business.pinterest.com/en/creating-your-account and applying for an account there. You can either start a new account for your business, or simply change your personal account to a business account.

One note on personal vs. business accounts: If you

choose to make your personal account into your business account, make sure you actually make your account look professional.

- Create (or rename) boards in ways that people will search for them. Make sure you use keyword-rich board descriptions (but don't go overboard and keyword stuff them! Pinterest looks at that as spamming.)

- Create a professional profile page, with a photo of yourself or your brand logo. Include a link to your website (if you have one). And use a keyword-rich description of your business and/or what you do.

- Get your website verified (see https://help.pinterest.com/en/business/article/claim-your-website)

- Sign up for Rich Pins, if you have a blog. (See https://business.pinterest.com/en/rich-pins)

Once you've done all of the above, it's time to start pinning affiliate links!

Because these things change, over time and on different platforms (like desktop vs. tablet, etc.) I'm just going to describe how you actually create affiliate pins in general.

Start by clicking the "create a new pin" button (typically found on the top-right of the screen.)

From there you will upload you pin image, write a (keyword-rich) title and description (remember to disclose that it's an affiliate link in the description), possibly add a few hashtags to your description, and finally add your affiliate link in the link section.

Once that's all done, simply save your new pin to your most relevant board first. If you can pin it to other boards, as well, I suggest using a pin scheduling tool like Tailwind. That way you don't pin the same image to a bunch of boards, all at one time. Rather, they'll be spaced apart by time, just like your other scheduled pins.

That said, this is a good time to say that, while you may be so excited right now, and just start thinking that you can pin affiliate links all day and get rich! The fact is that Pinterest doesn't officially have any rules about how many pins you can create per day... But I've personally noticed that if I make more than one or two affiliate pins per day, Pinterest seems less likely to share them, and *probably* considers them spam.

I can't prove that for sure, but it sure felt that way when I first discovered the fact that you could pin direct affiliate links.

Some days I'd create 10-15 affiliate pins... But hardly anyone was seeing them, much less clicking on them. I'd like to say I took it as a lesson and just started making fewer affiliate pins. But the truth is, I just got disheartened by putting in all that work, only to see it flop – HARD.

It wasn't until a few months later when I decided to just add one or two affiliate pins (when I had little blocks of time to do something quickly) that I noticed 1-2 affiliate pins per day did MUCH better that 10-15.

I also want to mention that Pinterest is a slow burn. 99.99% of the time, it will take months before you start seeing any "real" traffic from your pins. That may seem like a long time, but once your pins start picking up steam, you'll be so glad you stuck with it.

(I think the same thing goes for blogging in general. Most people need six months to a year to see any real growth or income. But it's worth it in the long run!)

If you'd like to learn more about promoting your blog and/or affiliate links on Pinterest, I have a (free for a limited time) class about that, that you can take here: https://thrivingaffiliates.com/recommends/pinterest/

But before we move on to the next chapter, I do want to mention one more thing: if you're blogging about something (or things) and your *blog post* includes affiliate links, you don't need to disclose the affiliate links in the pin descriptions. (But do be sure to include affiliate disclosures on your blog posts/pages.)

It's only when linking *directly* to an affiliate link that you need to disclose the fact that it's an affiliate link. Some people get tripped up on that. So I wanted to make sure it was clear.

Chapter 12 - Evergreen vs Limited Time Affiliate Promotions

I would guess that most affiliate marketers sign up for and promote "evergreen" products. Those are products (or services) that are for sale year-round.

But there are also affiliate marketers making six-figure commissions with limited-time affiliate promotions: products or services that go up for sale just once or twice a year. While I can't guarantee those types of numbers (or any income, really!) I think it's important to know the difference between Evergreen and Limited time promotions, and how to approach them.

One example of an evergreen product is a book. You could read and review a book, write a blog post about it, and (as long as the book was still valid, not something like

"Blogging in 2017") you could promote that post, year after year and make affiliate commissions on it.

An "internet famous" example of a limited time affiliate launch would be Marie Forleo's B-School. Once a year she launches B-School and affiliates clamor for the 50% commissions (the prices goes up from time to time, but typically the affiliate commissions are about $1000 per referral.)

Marie's affiliates are smart and many of them "sweeten" the deal, by offering their own programs for free to anyone who purchases through their affiliate link. In B-School's case, this is perfectly fine (and may even be encouraged!) I personally bought B-School through a woman who was offering her own $1000 money bootcamp course as a bonus.

I also knew that many other B-School affiliates would offer their own bonuses, so I "shopped around" and found the bonus that was most attractive to me. Because B-School is so popular, and is only available once a year, many other buyers/students like me do the same "bonus" shopping when the carts open.

So, as you can see, you'll need to approach these

different types of affiliate programs, well, *differently!*

Evergreen

Evergreen affiliate products are more on the passive side. You do the work up front, and then earn commissions (for months or years!) down the road.

The thing is, if you're promoting an evergreen product, you could also offer a bonus. In fact, offering a "limited time" free bonus when they buy through you is a great way to give people a sense of urgency and get them to buy today, rather than next week (or never, if they simply forget about it later!)

There are several types of software that can set up these limited time bonuses fairly easily. If you don't feel confident in setting it up yourself, you can always hire this task out. Once it's done and set up, you just need to get potential buyers to the web page.

But you can also promote one evergreen product in a variety of ways. I covered some of these ideas in Chapter six, but let's talk about some of those and more...

Reviews

Reviews are one of the most popular ways to

promote affiliate products. Any product, physical or digital, can be reviewed by you. One of the reasons these types of posts are so popular is because, many times, when someone is looking to buy a particular thing, they want to know they're making a smart purchase.

So, say I wanted to buy a set of pots and pans. It's not a huge investment, but it wouldn't be a cheap investment, either. I might have an idea of what I want. My mom always had Farberware, and it seemed to last a lifetime, but she bought hers in the 1980s, so I go to the web and search "Farberware reviews"… and that's where *your* review shows up!

Of course, if you don't blog about kitchenware, it could be about anything: clothes, shoes, online courses, books, travel, diapers, coffee, tools, home décor, etc.

How to

I'll admit: I don't like how to's as much as reviews for promoting most affiliate products. Why? Well, think about when a person searches for a review versus 'how to' use a thing. Usually, if they're searching for reviews, they haven't purchased it yet.

But if they want to learn how to use a particular thing (like a tablet, curling iron, piece of software, etc.), they probably already own it. But then again... Not always!

There are cases where how to's are perfect! Like in the case of crafts, woodworking projects, recipes, etc. In those cases, your readers may not have all, or any, of the products needed to create whatever it is you're showing them.

Demonstration Videos

These can fall under the "how to" category, just on video rather than a blog post. Again, think about the person's intention before spending time and effort into these videos.

Do they already own the product? If so, it might not be worth your time. (Unless you're promoting some sort of add-on or accessory.)

But if you're demonstrating how to clean an old stain 3 different ways (with affiliate links for each product) you have a much better chance of making affiliate sales over someone who searched for "how to clean hot coffee from carpet" (as the spill is likely fresh and they're not going to order a product and wait two to seven days for it to arrive).

Before you buy...

One way to attract buyers is by writing posts about what to know "before you buy." That way, they're closer to making a purchase and don't already own the item.

For example, Instant Pots® have been a craze on Pinterest for a while now. I caved and bought one myself. But there were at least two things I didn't realize when I bought it! One was that it's kind of just a pressure cooker (though some can be used more like a crockpot/slow cooker, too.)

I also didn't realize that, when they say it takes 1 minute to steam broccoli in my Instant Pot®, that's not including the time it takes to build up pressure in the pot (usually an additional 10-20 minutes.)

These kinds of tips or information are definitely helpful for someone looking to buy, and when you provide it to them, they just might buy through your affiliate link!

Best of...

Lists of "the best X" are extremely popular, and therefore sometimes hard to rank in Google for. But if you are in a small niche, it might be easier.

People searching for the best X (razor for sensitive skin, vacuum for hardwood floors, brush for curly hair, weights for women over 50, etc.) are almost always on their way to buying. If you can provide honest, thorough reviews of the best products in any given niche, you're attracting those people ready to buy.

Of course, these types of posts take time, and honesty... if you haven't actually used a particular product in the list, you might want to mention it, but also why you've included it.

There are exceptions (as there are with most of these post ideas.) Say you wanted to create a list of "the best wedding dresses for winter brides". Obviously this is not a situation where you'll have personally worn each of the dresses. In fact, this kind of post probably fits more accurately in the next promotion type.

Round Up

Round ups are a fun and easy way to put together a list of products in a related niche. I talked in depth about these in chapter six, but think of ideas like:

- 10 Yoga Mats for Hot Yoga Lovers
- 7 tools every blogger should have in their toolkit
- 19 pink home décor items
- 8 funny coffee mugs
- The Best Honeymoon Locations for Millennials
- Etc.

Gift Guides

Gift guides are basically like round ups, but with the intention of gift ideas for a particular person, like:

- Gifts for New Moms
- Gifts for Tween Girls
- Gift Ideas for Crafters
- Gifts for the Dad Who Has Everything
- Gift ideas for that person you just started dating
- Etc.

Gift guides are fun and tend do well on Pinterest. You can even create gift guides around: holidays, birth months, birth stones, birth signs, ages, genders, careers, hobbies, brands, relationships, pop culture, trends and more.

If you have a gift guide that is popular year after year, you can even update it from time to time. For example, if products sell out or are discontinued, if a more popular or updated item becomes available, etc. Keep the content fresh, because if they click through to buy and the product is no longer available, they'll likely be bummed and think of your site and/or content as stale and old.

Interview

If you can somehow interview a person or people around the product you're promoting, that's awesome!

I think of Pat Flynn of the Smart Passive Income Podcast interviewing the owner/creator of ConvertKit, an email marketing solution software. Pat has mentioned that, even though Nathan Barry wasn't on his show to pitch ConvertKit to Pat's audience, that interview has nonetheless resulted in many affiliate sales for Pat.

I've done similar interviews in the past with Etsy sellers and artists. Etsy has an affiliate program, so I would simply sprinkle images (with affiliate links) of their handmade goods throughout the blog interview.

If you blog about travel, you could interview people who stayed at a hotel you're an affiliate for.

If you blog about weddings, you could interview couples who had a destination wedding at a spot you're an affiliate for.

If you're a mommy blogger, you could even interview other moms about their favorite diapers (or cleaning supplies or instructive toys or favorite games for 4th graders or whatever it may be) and you could include links to all of their favorites.

I think you get the idea. It's free press for them (most people wouldn't say no to that!), and affiliate content for you!

Add Links to Existing Content

If you already have a blog or website and haven't yet tried using affiliate marketing as stream of income, one of the best places to start is in the blog posts you already have.

If you have a lot of content, as I mentioned before, you can use Google analytics (if you have it set up – and you should! It's free!) to find out what your most popular blog posts are. From there, take the top ten and, starting at the top, look for ways you can insert affiliate links.

Then you can repeat this process with your tenth to twentieth most popular posts, and so on.

If you're a new blogger and only have 10 posts or so, go through all of them and see where you can logically add affiliate links.

Resource Page

Having a resource and/or "tools" page is another (often overlooked or underutilized) place to include affiliate links. Usually blogs are in some sort of niche, and when people come to read them, they want to know more about that niche specifically!

Refer to chapter six for more resource page ideas.

Email Series and/or Email Marketing

As with all of my ideas, be sure you're allowed to use affiliate links in your emails before trying this idea. (Amazon says it's a no-no, while many other affiliate programs encourage it.)

But back in Chapter Six I mentioned starting an email list. I'd call this a vital step in building your blog and/or online business. Google and Pinterest and social media can all change their algorithms and overnight your business can change because of it (been there!)

But you OWN your list. Even if your email marketing software company goes under, you still own your list. You can simply move it to another email marketing company.

Plus, email marketing is more effective than social media marketing, or ads to a cold market.

What I like to do is have a series of welcome emails, some of which will have affiliate links in them. My welcome series looks like this:

- Welcome to the list, here's what to expect from me… (no affiliate links)

- Here's a little bit about me (no affiliate links)

- Here are my 5 favorite tools for XYZ (affiliate links)

- A freebie (affiliate links)

- More about my business (no affiliate links)

My welcome series continues to grow as I discover

new ways to connect with, and yes, *sell* to my audience. Yours can, too!

In addition to the welcome series, I also send out a weekly email newsletter. If weekly feels like too much to you, try to create a schedule you can work with. Maybe every two weeks, or, at the very least, once a month.

Lead Magnets

I talked about creating a lead magnet to attract email subscribers, but you can add affiliate links in your lead magnet itself, too!

Podcast

If you have a podcast you can mention affiliate products and use a link shortener (if allowed) so people can easily remember your link. Like www.YourDomainName.com/AffiliateName

You can also insert the affiliate links in your podcast show notes. As always, you should disclose the fact that those are affiliate links. It's as easy as saying something like:

"I love xyz brand, and I think you will, too! Use my

affiliate link, YourDomainName.com/AffiliateName and give a try for free for 14 days!"

YouTube Video

Depending on the nature of your YouTube Videos, you can use affiliate links in a variety of ways. You could do something similar to the podcast suggestion above.

Or, say you were doing a makeup tutorial (or other DIY, tutorial, demo, etc.), you could say something like, "I'll include my affiliate links to all the products I'm using today in the descriptions below this video!"

Pinterest

I wrote a whole chapter (eleven) on using affiliate links on Pinterest, but I think it bears repeating. Plus, you not only want to create affiliate pins and link directly to affiliate links, but using Pinterest to promote your blog, shop, or online business is a great way to get more traffic.

In fact, I like to create as many traffic sources as possible. That way, if one craps out on me, I can still rely on traffic from the other sources.

Social Media

I will admit: I haven't had much personal success selling on social media. But don't let my story stop you from trying! Because there are others out there (like influencers small and large!) who are killing it on platforms like Instagram.

And some people still swear by Facebook (pages or groups) for marketing on social media.

Even Twitter still has a (small but loyal) group of businesspeople who love (and effectively use!) the platform.

My thought about using affiliate links on social media is: if you want to do it and figure out a way to make it worth your time, by all means, go for it! But on the other hand, if it sounds terrible and you have no interest in it, then simply skip it. You'll want to put more focus on SEO (for Google, Pinterest, and/or YouTube), instead.

Limited Time Affiliate Promotions

While evergreen promotions can be more passive, limited time affiliate programs (also call "launches") can be super lucrative after a big push.

Typically, if you're going to promote a launch like this, you'll want to know well in advance of the "open cart" dates, so you can plan a detailed promotion period.

Obviously when the cart is open (this can vary from a few days to about two weeks, typically) you'll want to be in full promotion mode, sending out emails, posting about it on social media, talking about it on your podcast, etc.

But even before the cart opens, you might want to start talking (ie., blogging, podcasting, emailing, being active on social media, etc.) about related subjects, so the topic of whatever it is you'll be promoting will be on the minds of your people.

Let's take Amy Porterfield as an example. If you don't know her, she has an amazing podcast called Online Marketing Made Easy. She also has a course she launches once (or maybe twice) a year all about creating a course to sell online.

If I were one of her affiliates, I'd be talking about creating and selling courses for weeks ahead of the launch. I would write about the benefits of creating your own course, passive income streams, maybe interview a few course creators, ideally I'd even interview Amy herself. If I couldn't interview Amy, I'd "introduce" her to my audience in other ways, so that she herself was on their radar, too.

All of these things will plant the seeds in the minds of your readers... Thoughts like "selling a course could make me passive income", "course creation doesn't have to be hard", "I'm an expert enough to create a course," "Amy Porterfield knows all there is about successfully creating and selling online courses."

That way, by the time the cart opens, my audience has been warmed up to all of these ideas.

If you like the idea of limited time launches, but you aren't in the business/blogging niche, check out Ultimate Bundles, as they have limited time launches for several different product bundles, in a variety of niches, like heath & wellness, parenting, personal finance, self-care, DIY and creativity, and, yes, blogging and online business (and more!)

You can take a look at Ultimate Bundles and sign up their affiliate program at https://thrivingaffiliates.com/recommends/ub2/ (and yes, that is my affiliate link.) 😉

Chapter 13 – Pitfalls to Avoid

I definitely don't want to scare you off with this list of pitfalls to avoid with affiliate marketing, because there are quite a few. On the contrary, what I really want to do is to give you a heads up about these pitfalls so you can go into this business confidently! So, in no particular order:

Don't Break the Rules.

This may seem obvious, but so many bloggers and niche site owners just scroll through the affiliate terms and policies, click that little "accept" button, and start promoting!

When they do that, they might miss out on vital information that may either stop them from being accepted in the first place, or being removed as an affiliate, even after months or years of a successful affiliate partnership.

Can you image earning hundreds or thousands of dollars a month from an affiliate partnership, and have it taken away in an instant because you didn't fully read and/or follow the rules? What a bummer.

I wouldn't know little (but vital!) things like: you can't promote direct Etsy affiliate links on Pinterest, or you can't promote Amazon links in emails or PDFs, etc., if I didn't thoroughly read the rules of each program I join.

Again: I don't want you to be scared off by this, I want you to be empowered by it.

Getting Accepted or Rejected into an Affiliate Program

If, for some reason, you are rejected from any affiliate program: first, don't take it personally. Sometimes it's the smallest thing or things you need to change to be accepted. Other times the company simply isn't accepting new applicants at that time.

So if you're rejected, you'll want to know why. Politely reach out to the person who sent the rejection and ask why, and what you might be able to do to be accepted. Sometimes you'll never hear back. But most of the time you will, and then you can see if you can do things in order to re-apply and finally get into the program!

This actually happened to a couple of my friends. One got a response that her blog was simply too new. She added several more blog posts, let some time go by and reapplied — and she was approved!

The other didn't have the required affiliate disclosures, a privacy policy, etc. She fixed that, reapplied and was also then accepted.

So don't take your rejection as final. Find out what you need to do, do it, and re-apply.

Forgetting to Add Disclosures and Disclosure Pages

As I just mentioned in the last section, it's vital that you have the proper disclosures on your site.

I discussed earlier how you must have those FTC disclosures on every/any page with affiliate links (and don't think this applies just to US-based businesses! See www.termsfeed.com/blog/affiliate-disclosure for more information.) But you also need full pages on your site that may include (but are not limited to): affiliate disclosures/disclaimers, a privacy policy, terms & conditions, and any other legal disclaimers.

This may seem like a daunting task, and on your own it would be. But you can hire an attorney to help you write these. Or you can use a resource like the one I recommend at www.thrivingaffiliates.com/recommends/website-legal-templates

Failing the Kid (Or Grandma) Test

Listen, this next piece of advice is really just that: advice. It's not a hard and fast rule, and you won't lose your business if you don't follow it. But it's something that I like to follow, and if you've read this far, I think you will too. (No judgement from me if you don't, though!)

That is this: when deciding what affiliate programs to join and promote, ask yourself, "Would I be proud to share this with my kid (or niece/nephew/etc.)?" If you don't have kids, maybe the question is: "Would my Grandma be proud of me for promoting this offer?" If the answer is no to either one, then you might not want to do it.

Of course, everyone will have a different line in the sand regarding this point. My thought is that you probably don't want to promote something that, in your heart of hearts, no matter how big the affiliate commission is, you don't feel good about being an affiliate for.

I'll also say this: almost every single affiliate marketer has fallen into this trap before. I certainly have! There was a program that virtually promised to make me money, and the guy selling it had the fancy car and house, and well, I fell for it. I paid a thousand dollars for the program and quickly realized it was just a course that taught you how to sell his course.

It didn't really teach you about how to succeed with affiliate marketing in general. Just how to sell his course. Luckily I asked for a refund, and while at first they tried to deny the refund, I was tenacious and finally got it. But I can only imagine how many people weren't as lucky as me, and simply lost that money.

Don't get me wrong: I'm sure there are/were people making money with his "system", it just wasn't something that I aligned with.

That's the real message I want you to hear: just make

sure you (and your website/blog) are truly aligned with any affiliate program you choose to promote.

Don't Sign up for a Bunch of Programs at Once

This is another pitfall I've learned from experience. You might be so excited to get started making money with affiliate marketing, and say you join an affiliate network and you see all these offers that would be perfect for your target market!

You might be tempted to sign up for all of them right away! The downside to this is that you might just forget about some or all of them and then never actually promote them on your website.

What I like to do instead is keep track of the programs I might want to promote. I keep a list, and when I need new content ideas, etc., I'll go to that list and see which ones seem most appealing to my target market.

From there I'll choose one or two and start creating a list of keywords and/or blog post topic ideas I could write about and promote the products they offer.

While I don't want to just sign up for dozens of

programs too far in advance, I also don't want to wait to sign up for these programs when I'm desperate for content. So I usually start this process 4-6 weeks before I even plan on producing content around them.

Using Banners vs. Contextual Links

Just so we're clear: banners are those ad images you see on websites, and contextual links are affiliate links within the text of a blog post.

While visual ads/banners may have their place on your website, contextual links are likely to far outperform them.

In addition to links in text, I also recommend linking any product images with your affiliate link as well. People will click text links, but they often click on images, too. If that click leads to nowhere, you may have just lost a potential affiliate commission.

Speaking of Ads...

Some people use ads on their blogs right away. Others wait until they have 5000, 25,000, or even 100,000 sessions per month. And others still never put ads on their sites at all.

This is a personal preference, and it's one that you'll have to decide for yourself. My suggestion is, if you're even remotely interested in using ads, test them and see.

Some things you might want to consider are:

- Do my affiliate sales go down if I'm using ads?

- Does my site speed slow down too much when I'm using ads?

- Do ads make my site look "busy" or cluttered? Do I care?

I have ads on some sites and none on others. Besides just a personal preference thing, it also depends on each site's audience. They may or may not react to ads the way you expect. That's another reason I suggest testing.

The ad network I currently recommend most is at www.thrivingaffiliates.com/recommends/ezoic/ but you'll need at least 25,000 visitors to your website monthly. In the meantime, if you'd like to try ads, the old standard is Google Adsense.

Your Mindset

Unfortunately, your mindset about all of this can

also be a pitfall.

First, don't let anyone ever convince you that affiliate marketing is dead (far from it!) Or a scam (let them tell that to Amazon – quite possibly the most well-known ecommerce site on the planet – who has an affiliate program, or the New York Times, who make money with affiliate links.)

But as I mentioned in the intro, for most people, making money with affiliate marketing takes time. You might get your first sales within the first 2-3 months for just a few dollars and get excited. But if you're only making $20 a month after 6-8 months, that could be very discouraging for many people.

In fact, I see it all the time. People will put months and months into their blog and/or niche site, only to quit – potentially right before their businesses take off!

Sure, there are instances where people just chose the wrong niche. Or no niche at all. And their businesses were destined to fail.

But if you've read this far, I don't think that's you. You follow through. You get things done. You complete the task.

So if it takes 12 months to see $100 in revenue, or 24 months to see $1000, the key is to stick with it.

It takes time: for you to build up your content, for Google and other search engines to start ranking your site, and for your other promotional methods (like Pinterest) to begin to be truly effective.

Some sites will grow much more quickly, and others will take longer. But if you can (eventually) make $1000, $5000, $10,000 or even more per month, won't that be worth it? Especially if you're only working on your site 10-20 hours a week?

I think so. In fact, I know so. Earning money with affiliate marketing, especially when your site is about something you truly enjoy and/or is actually helping other people in the world... and, well, that's one of the most gratifying things you can ever do in life.

The end... almost!

Reviews are not easy to come by.

As an independent author with a tiny marketing budget, I rely on readers, like you, to leave short, honest reviews on Amazon.

Even if it's just a sentence or two!

So if you enjoyed the book, please leave a brief (or detailed!) review on Amazon.

I'm very appreciative for your review as it truly makes a difference.

Thank you from the bottom of my heart for purchasing this book and reading it to the end! I wish you all the success in affiliate marketing, and beyond!

References

Affiliate Marketing Definition, 9/3/2019, https://www.lexico.com/en/definition/affiliate_marketing

Influencers, are your #materialconnection #disclosures #clearandconspicuous?, 9/4/2019, https://www.ftc.gov/news-events/blogs/business-blog/2017/04/influencers-are-your-materialconnection-disclosures

WHAT ABOUT AFFILIATE OR NETWORK MARKETING?, 9/4/2019, https://www.ftc.gov/tips-advice/business-center/guidance/ftcs-endorsement-guides-what-people-are-asking#affiliateornetwork

Backlinko Nofollow Definition, 9/25/2019

https://backlinko.com/nofollow-link

Email ROI, 10/23/2019,

https://optinmonster.com/double-optin-vs-single-optin-which-one-is-better/

Affiliate Disclosures for non-US based bloggers, 1/10/2020,

www.termsfeed.com/blog/affiliate-disclosure

Website Legal Templates, 1/10/2020,

www.thrivingaffiliates.com/recommends/website-legal-templates/

Recommended Ad Network, 1/10/20,

https://thrivingaffiliates.com/recommends/ezoic/

www.ingramcontent.com/pod-product-compliance
Lightning Source LLC
Chambersburg PA
CBHW052350220526
45465CB00003BA/1037